2nd Edition

Failure Management & Success Management

Systematically managing the benefits of failure and the harms of success

Junesoo Lee
Paul Miesing
Seung-Joo Lee
Kwon Jung

KONG & PARK

PARKYOUNG
publishing&company

Preface

It is hard to define success and failure easily. This is not only because each person has different criteria for judging success and failure, but also because there are two paradoxes: The first paradox is that failure can beget a success in the future. The second paradox is that success can lead us to a failure. We encounter and respond to these two paradoxes in our daily lives. If we cannot perfectly avoid living in this paradox and irony of success and failure, how can we respond more actively to these paradoxes?

As an attempt to answer the above question more systematically, this study has been conducted since 2010. The authors used the grounded theory approach to analyze many cases and prior studies, and thereby we wanted to find common concepts and systematic patterns of dimensions in the data. As a result of the analysis, we created and proposed two concepts: Failure Management (FM) and Success Management (SM). In short, failure management is 'the method of systematically recognizing and using the benefits of failure, and success management can be defined as 'the method of systematically recognizing and preventing the harmfulness of success (i.e., the state in which reality is inferior to the goal or expectation).'

Through the above work, the authors published three articles over the years through Organizational Dynamics, an English academic journal (SSCI) that focuses on the readers such as management leaders, practitioners and MBA students. This book is a compilation of the three published papers and an additional chapter for readers who have little chance to access academic journals.

The contents presented in this book are common sense that has already been widely discussed by many scholars and front-line managers and experienced by ordinary people. Rather, the biggest advantage of the framework presented in this book would be the words 'failure management' and 'success management.' Even if you don't know or remember the specific principles or examples of the framework introduced in this book, it would be beneficial just to remember and live with the two new terms, 'failure management' and 'success management.' Because these terms provide a new lens or frame for us to look at the world.

This study was conducted mainly on cases in the field of enterprise management, but we believe that the framework of failure management and success management will be applicable in various fields of individuals and society. We hope this book will be a small reference for those who pursue 'dynamic sustainability through paradoxes.'

Acknowledgment

The research in chapters 2 and 3 of this book was conducted with the support of the Ministry of Education of the Republic of Korea, the National Research Foundation (NRF−2016 S1A3A2924956), and the KDI School of Public Policy and Management. The research in Chapter 4 and 5 was conducted with the support of the KDI School.

I would like to express my gratitude to the editors and the anonymous reviewers of Organizational Dynamics and also to Pakyoung−sa for allowing the publication.

I truly appreciate Reverend Kwak Sun−Hee for inspiring failure management and success management, my beloved family members for showing me the model of failure management and success management in real life, teachers, colleagues, and everyone who shared wisdom at many seminars.

Junesoo Lee,
on behalf of the authors

Table of contents

CHAPTER 01

How entrepreneurs can benefit from failure management

• • • Junesoo Lee, Paul Miesing

Paradox Management: Challenges and alternatives of organizations' failure-success management

••• Junesoo Lee

01 How entrepreneurs can benefit from failure management*

Junesoo Lee, Paul Miesing

BENEFITING FROM BUSINESS FAILURES

Can entrepreneurs benefit from failure? If so, more proactively, how can they use failure systematically? This paper studies this simple question. In order to answer the question, we begin introducing the existing ideas on failure that abounds in at least four categories: 1) why we learn from failure; 2) how we learn from failure; 3) what we learn from failure retrospectively; and 4) how we use failure prospectively. We then present detailed research questions designed to fill gaps in existing ideas on failure management.

---

* To cite the original manuscript of this chapter, use this reference: Lee, J., & Miesing, P. (2017). How Entrepreneurs Can Benefit from Failure Management. *Organizational Dynamics*, 46(3), 157 – 164.
https://doi.org/10.1016/j.orgdyn.2017.03.001.

Why We Learn from Failure

No matter how well organizations are managed, some failures are inevitable and even seemingly ubiquitous. According to the U.S. Census Bureau data, every year 470,000 businesses fail while a smaller number of businesses (400,000) newly start. Such high odds of entrepreneur failures are not so different across industries—no industry has more than a sixty percent survival rate after the first four years.

With business failures expected, the assertion that we can learn from failure is prevalent among numerous management scholars and practitioners. Simply put, failure teaches us what works and what does not. In other words, failures challenge underlying flaws in causality of organizational processes, and thereby lead to more accurate way of doing. Considering our bounded rationality, such learning from failure through ex-perimental approach might be the only way to learn about causal relationships.

As a result of such learning, organizational performances have often been improved by investigating and learning from failures. In detail, failures may help improve process reliability, reduce failure-related costs, and also improve the composition of the portfolio of projects through trial-and-error learning. So much prescriptive advice has been suggested to see failure as an important ingredient of the innovation process. In short, learning is more effective in failure than in success. While success can make decision makers remain where they are, failures can help renew their own strategic directions and practices.

How We Learn from Failure

Despite much evidence that we can learn from failure, the outcomes of learning from failure may vary according to different learning conditions. The learning conditions can be categorized in the following three ways: process of learning; facilitators of learning; and barriers of learning.

First, *process of learning* is crucial to successful learning from failure. This can be approached in the course or procedure of knowledge generation. Focusing on the procedure of knowledge generation, there are three stages of learning from failure: identifying failure; analyzing failure; deliberate experimentation. Besides such organizational processes of learning, the psychological and cognitive nature of learning from failure should be also considered because emotion is strongly involved in the process of recognizing and acknowledging failure.

Second, what are the *facilitators of learning* from failure? We can learn from failure by fostering an organizational system and culture that favors experimentation. Systemically, strategic management using formal planning system can be useful to deal with environment upheavals. From a cultural aspect, learning through failure or adversities can be achieved by being sensitive to warning signs of decline, normalizing failure, or facilitating improvisation, i.e., developing heuristic contingency plans.

Third, *barriers of learning* are also an important part of learning from failure. For instance, there are four barriers to learning from failure: technical; social; individual; and organizational. In detail, failures of 'learning from failure' are frequently witnessed due to incorrect inferences from small samples or noisy cues, or bias in interpreting causes of failure.

What We Learn from Failure—A Retrospective View

Lessons from failure feature not only failure process but also attribution of the causes of failure. Attribution is an attempt to trace back to the causes of events in order to understand the present and manage the future through corrective measures. In short, what we learn from failure is mainly about causes of failure so as to correct errors and not to repeat the same failures in the future. Hence, examining causes of failure is basically retrospective because it focuses on the past or root of failed event.

Then, what cause failure? According to two factors—1) if an action leading to failure is unguided or purposeful; 2) if the consequence of action is intended or not, there are four types of failure due to mechanical, accidental, intentional, and inadvertent causes. From other perspective as to causes of failure, failures can occur because of external or internal environments such as poor leadership, ignorance of organizational culture, unbalanced teamwork, or some unfit combination of leadership, capabilities and organizational design. As a provocative fact, entrepreneurs' incompetence or lack of experience may be a much more influential cause of failure than neglect, fraud, or disaster.

On the other hand, biased attributions have been often witnessed in many areas and disciplines. For instance, people tend to attribute their own success to themselves or internal factors, and their own failure to external factors. Conversely, managers tend to attribute others' success to external factors but their failure to internal factors.

How We Use Failure—A Prospective View

In contrast to the retrospective approach to causes of failure, another approach more emphatically focuses on the beneficial impacts of failed events. It should be noted that the retrospective and prospective perspectives on failure are not mutually exclusive because both are closely related to each other as retrospective correction of the past is also used for prospective planning for the future. However, the two views are distinguishable because of their different foci on failure. In other words, the prospective view on failure (regardless of its causes) pays more attention to how we can use failure in search for new opportunities.

TOWARD FAILURE MANAGEMENT

As reviewed earlier, most prior ideas on failure have a gap to be filled: *How we can use failure prospectively and systematically.* In other words, the existing research, theories, and even practical advices on the use of failure do not comprehensively explain prospective benefits from adversity within an integrated framework. Hence, the creative uses of failure are still left to hindsight or improvisation. However, systematic foresight on how we can take advantage of failure and adversity can be used not only as a theoretical framework but also as a heuristic for managerial and strategic decision making.

With this purpose in mind, this study provides a framework on 'how to learn from failure' in pursuit of 'how to use failure prospectively.' In this sense, this paper develops a failure management framework for creative decision making in paradoxical situations at both the individual and organizational levels in search for new insight on causes of failure and also new opportunities thanks to failure.

This study took multiple steps to answer the following questions:

1. *How are the major concepts such as 'failure' and 'failure management' defined operationally?* We begin with operationally defining the basic concepts of success and failure. As a new management perspective that takes advantage of failure, the concept of failure management is also introduced.

2. *What are the types of failure and is there any benefit to managing them?* We examined numerous examples and analyzed many studies to uncover the dimensions, categories, and concepts of a failure management framework. Through an iterative process of grounded theory that included inductive and deductive reasoning, we eventually identified three types of failure and six purposes to use failure advantageously that provided 16 propositions of failure management.

3. *What distinguishes failure management from other related management tools such as risk management and crisis management?* In order to infer the theoretical and practical contributions of failure management, we address the unique characteristics of our failure management framework by comparing it to other related management tools such as risk

management and crisis management which failure manage‑
ment is expected to complement.

A FRAMEWORK FOR FAILURE MANAGEMENT

Definitions and Concepts

Magnitude of event that is defined as failure can vary, for instance, in the forms of operational errors or mishaps, or catastrophe such as accidents, or plane crashes. Regardless of magnitude of failure, definition of failure may be in the eyes of beholder because there are usually various goals or references by which success or failure is judged. Setting an agreed‑upon organization goal or reference point is especially difficult because of political and narrative nature of the distinction between success and failure.

But such dynamics of establishing official or formal goals to define success and failure is beyond this study. Rather, we judge success or failure as the outcome from a black box in which actions are compromised and negotiated to set, achieve and evaluate a formal and fixed goal. Specifically, we operationally define success and failure as follows. (1) *Success* is 'a state where reality is superior to the goal.' (2) *Failure* is 'a state where reality is inferior to the goal.' According to this operational definition, in this study the word 'failure' means not only complete loss or bankruptcy but also any adverse state such as frustration, conflict, or regret in which reality is worse than expectations. Finally, (3) *failure management* is defined as 'the systematic ways to make the most from failure.'

As a result of the comprehensive sampling and analyses through grounded theory approach, two dimensions of a failure management framework were found. The first is the *types* of failure (and its side effects). According to the operational definition of failure (i.e., a state where reality falls short of the goal), there can be three different types of inferior reality in terms of internal/external resources or forces: *deficiency, excess,* and *inconsistency.* The second dimension we use is *purposes* to use failure. The first three purposes – *saving internal resources, reforming internal hazard,* and *learning new knowledge* – are the efforts to adapt the internal environment in the face of failure. The second four purposes – *learning new knowledge, discouraging external threats, attracting external supports,* and *complementing multiple forces* – are attempts to influence the external environment. Noteworthy is the fact that *learning* is shared by both internal and external adaptation because most learning from failure is shared by both internal and external stakeholders involved in the incident of failure.

We found that the three types of failure along with the six purposes to use failure can be combined into 16 potential benefits. In other words, there are 16 different ways organizations can respond to take advantage of adversity that comprehensively summarizes the propositions on the benefits of failure (see Appendix A.) Each of these propositions can be defined, described, and supported by examples as follows.

Propositions

> **⊗ Proposition 1**
>
> **Failure (deficiency, excess, or inconsistency) can function as a test bed under extreme condition.**
>
> Any type of failure provides extreme conditions in which certain variables' characteristics or attributes can be tested and learned by either internal or external stakeholders. Simply put, failure teaches about what does and what does not work. For instance, Silicon Valley's 'FailCon' (which means 'failure conference') has a new business model that helps entrepreneurs learn from failure. Apple's success is based on Steve Jobs' failures such as NeXT computer and iTunes phone which became the basis for the success of OS X(10) and iPhone, respectively. Encountering a big quality control problem in 2009, Domino Pizza dramatically grew after it issued a quick apology and undertook full-scale reform. Some premature SONY products such as its LED TV or PDA before the smartphone failed in terms of sales, but they played a role in familiarizing customers with such new devices and thereby increased their willingness to buy later. Immediately after Jaws Rice Cake, a restaurant chain in Korea, had many customer complaints in 2012 about an employee's

rude attitude, the CEO promptly posted an apology statement on its Webpage and promised a strict retraining of all employees. Such a swift and sincere response drew customers' attention and proved the restaurant's trustworthiness.

❯ Proposition 2

Deficiency can help save resources by forgoing an inferior opportunity.

A missed chance due to insufficient resources can actually help avoid chasing an inferior opportunity and thereby save resources. In general, late-movers have an advantage if they learn from the first mover's trials and errors. For instance, in the early 1950s Lockheed participated in a new bomber development project launched by DARPA but had to fund itself because it joined the project too late to get government grants. As a result, Lockheed was able to privatize all the technology developed in the middle of research that led to enormous profits from the new technology. More recently, although Samsung failed to set the world standard in a smart phone operating system (OS), by using Android it conserved and successfully reallocated resources to make more advanced communication devices.

Excess can help saving for a superior opportunity.

Surplus resources can be used for new purposes or hidden assets can be reevaluated and released to exploit new opportunities. Recently, New York City brought new life to an abandoned railroad track as an oasis of the city. The re-created railroad named 'the High Line' became not only a public park but also a new venue for children education, community building, and local economic growth. Similarly, Tropical Islands Resort in Germany was once an obsolete airship hangar of a bankrupt company that was reused as a famous indoor beach resort. The 'sharing economy' exemplified by Uber taxi and Airbnb is a new way to make the most of excess assets by facilitating direct transactions among individuals. The Kimpo airport of South Korea, once its largest, had seen customers dwindle after a new airport opened nearby so it used the excess space for a new shopping place to draw new customers.

» Proposition 4

Inconsistency can help conserve resources and spread risk.

Inconsistent patterns of resources or information can actually help reduce risk. For instance, diversifying products, customers, markets, suppliers, technologies, etc. are a hedge against unforeseen variability. Personnel policies that employ part-timers help employers save costs while also letting employees be flexible. When used appropriately, having a part-time workforce addresses such key staffing issues as covering hard-to-fill positions and helps recruit, retain, and engage valuable employees. In the best seller Nudge, the authors suggest 'nudging' to achieve non-forced compliance. They pointed out that, in the case of government, public relations subtly lead citizens in a certain direction, and although it does not guarantee consistent compliance of citizens as direct regulation does, it can be more efficient and effective because such indirect convincing of and communication with citizens can still help not only achieve guidance but also avert invading freedom of citizens. The benefit of inconsistency can be also witnessed in group management. Ambiguity (i.e., inconsistent orientation) of an alliance's goal can help retain the members in the alliance because an ambiguously-defined common goal can be interpreted and advocated in many ways that fit each member's own goal.

» Proposition 5

Deficiency can help improve effectiveness and efficiency.

Having insufficient resources can eliminate harmful or needless redundancy. One reason is that it rallies the troops. For instance, Komatsu entered the U.S. market in 1967 with its rallying cry of 'Maru-C' that roughly translated into English as 'Encircle Caterpillar!' the largest bulldozer maker. Similarly, during the widely known Cola Wars Pepsi had the mission to 'Beat

Coke.' Even after a business succeeds, it is quite worth proactively managing it by deliberately tightening its belt so that its success does not unwittingly encourage hubris. For instance, many industrial experts believe that Samsung's successive feats in business is due to its 'consistent sense of crisis' that forces constant vigilance and innovation. In fact, when Samsung earned the largest profits in its history in the first quarter of 2013, rather than celebrate this feat it emphasized the sense of crisis in the face of a turbulent global market. A new business introduced in the book Nudge, stickk.com, helps commit members to a specific action by forcing them to deposit some money that can be retrieved only after they achieve their agreed-upon resolutions.

⊗ Proposition 6

Excess can help stimulate innovation.

Trying to resolve a problem of 'embarrassment of riches' can actually be an impetus for innovation. A stretch goal, also called BHAG for 'Big Hairy Audacious Goals' because they are seemingly impossible to achieve, can be beneficial for organizational performance by facilitating the use of slack resources, spurring creativity and innovation, prompting new product development, and tightening the budget belt. A BHAG, which requires confidence, enhances team spirit and creates visionary goals by stressing high commitment and working outside of a comfort zone. In Built to Last, Collins and Porras argue that 'Good

Enough Never Is'. They also reject the idea of a 'finish line' and define a visionary company as one that is never satisfied with its results. For instance, Louis Vuitton eyeglass frames had to invent something new and unique to outdo the imitations and counterfeiting of other manufacturers.

» Proposition 7

Inconsistency can help challenge the status quo and avert bias.

An unstable environment helps maintain creativity and preparedness by preventing individuals from being stuck in inertia. In management, the beneficial impacts of inconsistency are often suggested as follows: Imbalance between clients' demands and revenue growth prompts companies to devise a wide range of strategies, conflict can be a seed for developing new knowledge, and destabilizing conditions help changes to emerge. The emergence of disruptive technology that drove the watch market to turbulence actually helped traditional mechanical watch manufacturers newly re-discover their market niche where it turned out there were quite a few customers who still prefer and cherish mechanical watches.

» Proposition 8

Deficiency can help reduce risk or external threats.

Deficient resources can allay opponents' willingness or capacity for depredation. Before Steve Jobs' premature death, iPhone 4S had been much criticized but Apple succeeded in deflecting such criticism and having Steve's death eclipse iPhone 4S problems. As a result, the sale of iPhone 4S actually exploded after his death. In 2012, Toyota pessimistically announced that it would sell less than ten million cars for that year which was much smaller than expected. But many industry analysts speculated that low-balling its sales estimate was an attempt to avert U.S. manufacturers' checks against Toyota.

» Proposition 9

Opponents' excess resources can help deepen their inertia or over-commitment.

Companies can go on the counter-offense by taking advantage of their opponents' excess momentum and the corresponding inertia or over-commitment. Take a martial art, judo, for instance. A heavier opponent can be thrown more easily by Judo using an opponent's weight and force against him or her. In business competition, just like judo, companies can beat rivals by taking advantage of the opponent's excess momentum and the corresponding inertia or over-commitment. Such principle of 'judo strategy' to use an opponent's inertia and over-investment was also recommended by the ancient Chinese warfare lessons in The Art of War.

» Proposition 10

Inconsistency can help discourage threat through instability.
An unstable condition or inconsistent and unreliable information can help remove undesirable or ineffective activity, behavior, or threat that is vulnerable to a changing environment. Behavioral economists have described such impact of inconsistency on human relations. For instance, inconsistent information in a message can confuse observers or recipients, causing them to blunder. Many nonprofit organizations actually use their tenuous financial situations as an excuse to have their ineffective board members resign voluntarily. Peace First (formerly Peace Games) had become conflicted over two inconsistent missions – developing college student volunteers and serving school kids. But in this wavering situation, it dropped its old mission and instead developed a new one to embrace more young adult volunteers and partners to work with schools to build safe, effective climates where children learn how to be engaged and active citizens. The organization now strives to teach students to become problem-solvers who will create social change. Another non-profit, Trinity Alliance in Albany, New York, faced an inconsistent management environment that served to stimulate and shake up its staff with some inactive and underperforming members departing.

❯ Proposition 11

Deficiency can help induce external help.

Insufficient resources can prompt the willingness of reciprocal help and attention from stakeholders. A recent human resource management study showed that employees with deficient capability tend to feel indebted and work harder than those with sufficient capabilities who can rather easily become complacent. Stephen Hawking confessed that his disorder helped his book sell more. Similarly, reverse psychology marketing arouses customers' curiosity with intentionally deficient information and 'Today only!' advertising that give the 'appearance of limitation' that incite a run on stores. A Japanese hotel used a provocative advertisement 'we are a cheapie' which attracted customers looking for a low-end product with low quality and low price. On the other extreme, some luxurious department stores adopt so-called 'secret marketing' that informs only a few prestigious customers of new product information. Such tactics help maintain the luxurious image of their business and also draw more attention from those who feel isolated from the marketing. Limited items are also often used as a powerful means of advertisement because scarcity implies prestigious value. Tim Cook, Steve Jobs' successor, took over a highly-successful Apple yet decided to shift its focus to low-end products such as the iPad mini in order to attract a wider range of customers.

» Proposition 12

Excess can help draw attention or meet new demands.

Things that are outrageous or edgy can help generate new interest but sometimes require slack resources. For instance, Samsung used Apple's lawsuits against it as an opportunity for buzz marketing. Such conflicts between Apple and Samsung made the general public recognize Samsung as a powerful competitor of Apple. Take another famous anecdote about the birth of Ivory Soap, supposedly invented by an engineer who mistakenly instilled too much air into soap in the production process. The result of such excess air bubbles was a soap that could float, which attracted new customers who preferred a lighter soap. Having a monopoly in a new product market can fail to interest customers because they hesitate to buy unique and untested products; rather, competing with additional manufacturers can familiarize customers with that item. On the other hand, you can sometimes draw more customers in fashion or luxury markets with higher prices for those engaging in 'conspicuous consumption.'

» Proposition 13

Inconsistency can help stimulate or vitalize support.

An unstable environment can be used to stimulate or vitalize some targets that support organizations. From a network point of view, turbulent environments can stimulate cooperation. The Kitchener-Waterloo region of Canada and the Oulu region of

Finland experienced surplus human resources due to, respectively, Blackberry's and Nokia's many layoffs that actually helped to stimulate the regional economy by launching many technology ventures.

⊗ Proposition 14
Deficiency can help get and nurture complementary forces.
Insufficient resources can help make room for other compensating resources or opportunities to grow and eventually prosper together. From an ecological point of view, some sacrifices are rather conducive to the sustainability of the overall environment and system. For instance, Japanese Keiretsu and Korean Chaebol business groups are known to cooperate to create shared value. These networks have averted collapse by accepting some short-term losses (i.e., profit-sharing) by forging long-term symbiosis between the conglomerates and the small- and medium-size contractors. Similarly, many neighboring competitors, especially in the restaurant business, do not compete themselves out of business because the marketing benefits of such a 'cluster' in attracting more customers to the area exceeds possible losses. In 2014, electric car manufacturer Tesla Motors decided to share its patents with other automobile producers in order to nurture the technological and market basis of electric cars. Such generous action also served to advertise Tesla's confidence about its technological competitiveness and leadership.

❱❱ Proposition 15

Excess can help check, eclipse, or unite against a threat.

It has been said that 'The enemy of my enemy is my friend.' A hostile environment can prompt collaboration among competitors, opponents, or even strangers when confronting a common threat. For instance, the US and the UK decided to ally with the Soviet Union during WWII because both recognized the need to defeat a common enemy, Nazi Germany. 'Dumping' is similar to an arms race because while it hurts short-term profits it ultimately defeats competitors. DIMBY ('Definitely in My Backyard') can also be explained by this logic since people are sometimes willing to attract unpleasant facilities to their community in order to prevent other more unpleasant facilities from being built. In 2012, Samsung welcomed the Korean government's restrictions on cell phone manufacturers' subsidies to customers because it would enervate a more vulnerable LG.

❱❱ Proposition 16

Inconsistency can help offset another inconsistency with an opposite pattern.

A loss due to oscillation can be compensated for by using another oscillation that has the opposite pattern. For instance, inherent risks of carrying an item that has seasonal sales (e.g., ski goods) can be averted by carrying another item with the opposite seasonal sales (e.g., tennis goods) yet serves the same customer base. Infosys, a global information technology company, has employed a 'Global Delivery Model' (GDM) to take advantage of the time lag between multiple offices in different countries to provide seamless 24-hour service to customers.

FAILURE MANAGEMENT VS. OTHER MANAGEMENT TOOLS

Besides the propositions of failure management stated above, why is it necessary to use a new concept of 'failure management' in the first place? In order to clarify the unique characteristics of failure management, the relationship between three management tools – risk management, crisis management, and failure management – can be summarized in Fig. 1 that shows various types of problems to be addressed in decision making.

All of these management tools are based on quite different goals and philosophies. Risk management is to review and revise errors with a retrospective view in order to predict and prevent them, and crisis management is to control and contain present failures. In other words, risk management and crisis management are *retrospective efforts to avert adversity* by analyzing the causes of failure, continuing to pursue the existing goal, and trying to survive in spite of failure.

On the contrary, *failure management is rather prospective* that

Figure 1 Failure management framework for prospective
          decision making

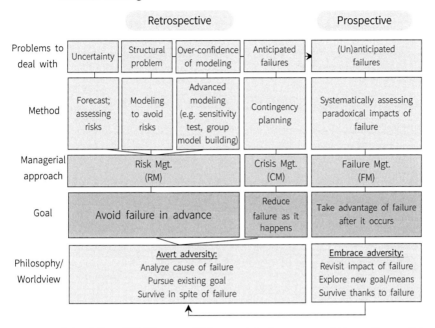

	Retrospective				Prospective
Problems to deal with	Uncertainty	Structural problem	Over-confidence of modeling	Anticipated failures	(Un)anticipated failures
Method	Forecast; assessing risks	Modeling to avoid risks	Advanced modeling (e.g. sensitivity test, group model building)	Contingency planning	Systematically assessing paradoxical impacts of failure
Managerial approach	Risk Mgt. (RM)			Crisis Mgt. (CM)	Failure Mgt. (FM)
Goal	Avoid failure in advance			Reduce failure as it happens	Take advantage of failure after it occurs
Philosophy/ Worldview	Avert adversity: Analyze cause of failure Pursue existing goal Survive in spite of failure				Embrace adversity: Revisit impact of failure Explore new goal/means Survive thanks to failure

Before Failure: RM & CM can use FM framework to discover any variables worth managing
After Failure: Once a new variable is discovered through FM, it can be managed by RM & CM

cherishes adversity by re-valuating failure, exploring new goals or means, and examining various strategic options to improve because of adversity. Such different features of each management tool do not imply that they are mutually exclusive in practice. Failure management can help risk management expand investment portfolios while also helping crisis management improve contingency planning by providing the systematic frameworks to find paradoxical impacts of failure worth managing.

CONCLUSION

Given risk now or in the future, what can entrepreneurs do? They can try to either reduce the possibility of failure retrospectively or capture new opportunities created by failure prospectively. But such a prospective approach to failure has been vaguely dealt with. Without an understanding of the systematic patterns of the benefits of failure, its paradoxical impacts would still be managed impromptu. So, this paper extends existing ideas of the prospective use of failures and thereby presents a framework for organizations to benefit from failure more reliably.

However, we cannot always benefit from failure. Of course, we are more familiar with failures that have no benefit. That is why each of the 16 propositions of failure management we propose in this paper were expressed with the words 'can help.' In other words, failure alone is not a sufficient condition for the corresponding paradoxical benefits. Seeing an opportunity is one thing, but actually exploiting it is another. Failures can be beneficial only when they are treated in a certain way. So the failure management propositions are at least the collections of the necessary but insufficient conditions for the benefits of failure.

We hope that the propositions and frameworks presented in this paper become the bases of future studies that will explore whether and how failure management can be practically used in actual organizational settings. In this spirit, we suggest the research questions for such future studies be about the drivers, strategic options, procedures, and preparedness of failure management.

SELECTED BIBLIOGRAPHY

For the original idea of failure management, see the work of the author: Lee, J. (2014). *Essays on Failure Management of Nonprofit Organizations.* Doctoral dissertation. University at Albany, State University of New York.

For 'why we learn from failure,' see: Haunschild, P. R., & Sullivan, B. (2002). Learning from complexity: Effects of prior accidents and incidents on airlines' learning. *Administrative Science Quarterly*, 47, 609 − 643; Sitkin, S. B. (1992). Learning through failure: The strategy of small losses. *Research in Organizational Behavior*, 14, 231 − 266; Baum, J. A., & Dahlin, K. (2007). Aspiration performance and railroads' patterns of learning from train wrecks and crashes. *Organization Science*, 18, 368 − 385; Henderson, A. D., & Stern, I. (2004). Selection−based learning: The coevolution of internal and external selection in high− velocity environments. *Administrative Science Quarterly*, 49, 39 − 75; Madsen, P. M. & Desai, V. (2010). Failing to Learn? The Effects of Failure and Success on Organizational Learning in the Global Orbital Launch Vehicle Industry. *Academy of Management Journal*, 53(3), 451 − 476.

For 'how to learn from failure,' see: Cannon, M. D., & Edmondson, A. C. (2005). Failure to Learn and Learning to Fail (Intelligently): How Great Organizations Put Failure to Work to Innovate and

Improve. *Long Range Planning*, 38, 299−319; Shepherd, D. A., & Cardon, M. S. (2009). Negative emotional reactions to project failure and the self-compassion to learn from the experience. *Journal of Management Studies*, 46(6), 923−949; Farjoun, M. (2002). Towards an Organic Perspective on Strategy. *Strategic Management Journal*, 23(7), 561−594; Amankwah-Amoah, J. (2016). An integrative process model of organisational failure. *Journal of Business Research*, 69(9), 3388−3397; Eriksson, K. & McConnell, A. (2011). Contingency planning for crisis management: Recipe for success or political fantasy? *Policy and Society*, 30(2), 89−99; Shepherd, D. A., Patzel, T. H., & Wolfe, M. (2011). Moving forward from Project Failure: Negative Emotions, Affective Commitment, and Learning from the Experience. *Academy of Management Journal*, 54(6), 1229−1259; Eggers, J. P. (2012). Falling flat: Failed technologies and investment under uncertainty. *Administrative Science Quarterly*, 57, 47−80; Baumard, P., & Starbuck, W. H. (2005). Learning from failures: Why it may not happen. *Long Range Planning*, 38, 281−298.

For 'what we learn from failure: retrospective view,' see: Weiner, B. (1985). An attributional theory of achievement motivation and emotion. *Psychological Review*, 92(4), 548−573; Stone, D. (2011). *Policy Paradox: The Art of Political Decision Making*. W. W. Norton & Company; Vaara, E. (2002). On the discursive construction of success/failure in narratives of post-merger integration. *Organization Studies*, 23(2), 211−248; Wagner, J. A., & Gooding, R. Z. (1997). Equivocal information and attribution: An investigation of patterns of managerial sensemaking. *Strategic Management Journal*, 18(4), 275−286.

For 'how to use failure: prospective view,' see: McGrath, R. G.

(2011). Failing by Design. *Harvard Business Review*, 89(4), 76−83; Beech, N., MacIntosh, R., Maclean, D., Shepard, J., & Stokes, J. (2002). Exploring Constraints on Developing Knowledge: On the Need for Conflict. *Management Learning*, 33(4), 495−512.

For BHAG, see: Collins, J., & Porras, J. I. (1994). *Built to Last: Successful Habits of Visionary Companies.* New York: Harper Business.

For 'judo management,' see: Yoffie, D., & Cusumano, M. (1999). Judo Strategy: The Competitive Dynamics of Internet Time. *Harvard Business Review*, 77(1), 70−81.

For 'Nudge,' see: Thaler, R. H., & Sunstein, C. R. (2008). *Nudge: Improving Decisions about Health, Wealth, and Happiness.* New York: Penguin Books.

Appendix A. Failure management propositions

Types of failure (and their side effects)	Purposes to use failure (i.e., benefits of failure)					
	Internal adaptation			External adaptation		
	Saving (internal resources)	Reforming (internal hazards)	Learning (new knowledge)	Discouraging (external threats)	Attracting (external supports)	Complementing (multiple forces)
Deficiency	#2: Forgo inferior opportunity and save resources. Example: Samsung using Android for its smart phone operating system	#5: Improve effectiveness and efficiency. Example: Komatsu's 'Maru-C' rallying cry and Pepsi's mission to 'Beat Coke'	#1: Failure (deficiency, excess, or inconsistency) can function as a test bed under extreme condition. Example: Silicon Valley's 'FailCon'	#8: Reduce risk or threat. Example: Toyota's pessimistic forecast	#11: Induce external help. Example: Japanese hotel advertising 'We are a cheapie.'	#14: Get and nurture complementary forces. Example: Japanese Keiretsu and Korean Chaebol
Excess	#3: Save surplus for superior opportunity. Example: Uber taxi and Airbnb	#6: Stimulate innovation. Example: BHAG		#9: Deepen opponents' inertia or over-commitment. Example: Judo strategy	#12: Draw attention or meet new demands. Example: Ivory Soap	#15: Check, eclipse, or unite against threat. Example: Samsung welcoming government's regulation
Inconsistency	#4: Conserve resources and spread risk. Example: diversification	#7: Challenge status quo and avert bias. Example: mechanical watch market re-discovered due to disruptive technology		#10: Discourage threat through instability. Example: Peace First's changed mission	#13: Stimulate or vitalize support. Example: Canada's Kitchener-Waterloo and Finland's Oulu	#16: Offset another inconsistency with opposite pattern. Example: Infosys 'Global Delivery Model'

Note: Propositions #1 – #16 are numbered in the cells.

Appendix B. Risk, crisis, and failure/success

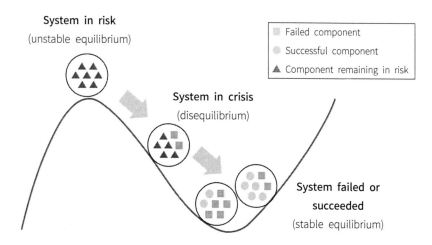

System in risk
(unstable equilibrium)

▨	Failed component
◕	Successful component
▲	Component remaining in risk

System in crisis
(disequilibrium)

System failed or succeeded
(stable equilibrium)

Note. Appendix B was not a part of the original manuscript.

The difference between failure management, risk management, and crisis management lies basically in the difference between risk, crisis, and failure/success. Using a graphic metaphor as Appendix B might be helpful to explain the different meanings of risk, crisis, and failure.

Here is a mountain. At the summit we have a ball which is a system containing seven independent or interconnected components. Our task is to roll the ball down while keeping the ball components as intact as possible. The ball at the summit remains in risk as it begins to roll down. So we can call this state 'unstable equilibrium.' Once this ball starts to roll down, some components begin to fail creating a system in crisis. It's obviously now in disequilibrium.

When this ball reaches the bottom and stops, the only course of action is to determine the success or failure of the system. The first ball at the bottom shows that five of the seven components failed, so this system failed as a whole. But the other ball at the bottom shows that only two of seven components failed, so we can conclude that this system is closer to success than the first one.

02 Making hindsight foresight*
: Strategies and preparedness of
failure management

Junesoo Lee

INTRODUCTION OF FAILURE MANAGEMENT

Failure can be beneficial. In other words, failure can help us make creative breakthroughs. But how? Let's think about the answers to the next questions. How did the United States use the threat of the USSR's achievements during the space race of the 1960s? How did the Post-it note of 3M that was too weak to permanently hold paper on a surface become so popular among consumers? How can you throw heavy opponents easily in judo? How did Apple spin Steve Jobs' death to be beneficial to the sales of iPhone 4S? In short, are there any systematic patterns through which we can

---

* To cite the original manuscript of this chapter, use this reference: Lee, J. (2018). Making Hindsight Foresight: Strategies and Preparedness of Failure Management. *Organizational Dynamics*, 47(3), 165 – 173. https://doi.org/10.1016/j.orgdyn.2017.12.002.

make creative strategies by using failure or adversity? This study attempts to answer this question.

Recently, the idea that failure can be a paradoxical seed for creating strategies has come to light. The idea of 'failure management' suggests that entrepreneurs actually have been using their failures and challenges beneficially to create new opportunities. Of course, failure is in the eye of the beholder. According to the expectations of each decision maker, the definition of failure may range from total loss or bankruptcy to frustration, conflict, challenge, regret, or any adversity. One of the common grounds of the diverse definitions of failure is the fact that failure is an adverse state in which reality is inferior to expectations.

ABOVE AND BEYOND FAILURE MANAGEMENT

According to the framework of failure management, there are 16 different ways in which organizations can benefit from their failures or adversities. These 16 ways encompass both retrospective and prospective activities in the face of failure. The retrospective approach to failure focuses on how to find and correct the causes of failure, which is a focus of risk management and crisis management. On the other hand, the prospective approach emphasizes more forward-looking ways to benefit from failure and create new opportunities. In sum, the failure management framework can help systematically describe and prescribe how organizations can use failures both retrospectively and prospectively by complementing risk management and crisis management.

However, the present framework of failure management does not specify the mechanisms behind the 16 propositions such as 1) either retrospective or prospective strategic options in the value chain of organization; 2) decision-making processes and preparedness of failure management. In light of this situation, a grounded theory approach was employed to explore the answers to the following two questions.

> *Q1. What strategies can we create to use failure retrospectively and prospectively?*
>
> *Q2. How can we assess how well we are prepared to use failure?*

With the goal of answering these two questions, the examples presented in the introduction will be analyzed again to better determine systematic patterns behind creative strategies and also how to be better prepared in the face of failure.

For this first question, we need to think about the two types of answers to the question "**Why** did we fail?" The first type of answer is retrospective: "We failed due to (or because of) a certain **past cause**." The second answer is instead prospective: "We failed due to (or for) a certain **future purpose**."

If you take the first answer, you will focus on how to correct past errors. But if you adopt the second answer, you will pay more attention to how to evaluate the failure from the perspective of the future. Then, how can we systematically analyze such different attributions of failure to make strategies more creative? There are some distinctive factors characterizing the retrospective and prospective strategies in the face of failure, as discussed below.

Factor One: How Do We Respond to Failure?

As the failure management framework suggests, failure can be operationally defined as 'a state in which reality is inferior to one's goals or expectations.' Such an inferior reality may occur in the forms of a deficiency, excess, or inconsistency. Based on the operational definition of failure, there are two ways to respond to failure (i.e., the case in which reality is inferior to one's goals). First, we can try to tune our reality to attain our goals. Second, we can try to adapt our goals to fit our reality.

Factor Two: What Opportunities Do We Get from Failure?

Besides the responses to failure noted above, opportunities from failure can occur in various ways. Considering various management activities that are conducted in the value chain of an organization, the benefits of failure may diffuse throughout the value chain. For instance, a failure in leadership can be beneficial to communication because a loss of leadership that had an entrenched network with outsiders can help diversify communication channels with external stakeholders. In another case, a failure in current customer relations can help facilitate new relations with the broader general public as new customers. In a nutshell, in order to help describe such difference between 'where failure occurs' and 'where opportunities occurs thanks to failure,' management activities in the value chain or organization can be categorized as follows.

Management activities in the value chain:
- Governance/leadership
- Internal human resources
- Planning/communication

- Physical capacity/assets
- Finance
- (Relations with) partners/contractors/suppliers
- (Relations with) customers
- (Relations with) the general public
- (Relations with) competitors
- (Relations with) regulators

In terms of these management activities in the value chain of an organization, there are two types of opportunity from failure. The first type of opportunity from failure is that we can improve our reality using failure as an impetus to change. This opportunity occurs in the same management activity in the value chain in which the failure occurs. The second type of opportunity from failure is that we can create new goals using failure as a door to new benefits. This opportunity occurs in a management activity in a value chain other than the one in which the failure occurs.

One example of the pattern in which benefits of failure diffuse to every corner of management activities in the value chain is listed in Table 1. This 10 × 10 symmetric square shows the relation between the two things—'where failure occurs' and 'where opportunities thanks to failure occurs' in the value chain of an organization. In this table, 'S' in the diagonal represents the case that opportunity thanks to failure occurs in the same value chain as

Table 1   Diffusions of benefits of failure in the value chain of an organization

Management activity where failure occurred	Management activity where opportunity occurred thanks to failure									
	Governance/leadership	Internal human resources	Planning/communication	Physical capacity/assets	Finance	(Relations with) partners /contractors/suppliers	(Relations with) customers	(Relations with) the general public	(Relations with) competitors	(Relations with) regulators
Governance/ leadership	S	D	D	D	D	D	D	D	D	D
Internal human resources	D	S	D	D	D	D	D	D	D	D
Planning/ communication	D	D	S	D	D	D	D	D	D	D
Physical capacity/ assets	D	D	D	S	D	D	D	D	D	D
Finance	D	D	D	D	S	D	D	D	D	D
(Relations with) partners/contractors/ suppliers	D	D	D	D	D	S	D	D	D	D
(Relations with) customers	D	D	D	D	D	D	S	D	D	D
(Relations with) the general public	D	D	D	D	D	D	D	S	D	D
(Relations with) competitors	D	D	D	D	D	D	D	D	S	D
(Relations with) regulators	D	D	D	D	D	D	D	D	D	S

Note. 'S' in the diagonal represents the case that opportunity thanks to failure occurs in the same value chain in which the failure occurs. 'D' represents the case the opportunity occurs in a value chain other than the one in which the failure occurs.

where the failure occurs, and 'D' represents the case in which the opportunity occurs in a value chain other than the one in which the failure occurs. In this way, this table exemplifies the patterns of how benefits of failure diffuse throughout the value chain of an organization.

Spectrum of Retrospective and Prospective Strategies of Failure Management

By using the two factors noted above (i.e., how we respond to failure; what opportunities we gain from failure), the scopes of retrospective and prospective strategies dealing with failure can be systematically described, as listed in Table 2. This table lists the spectrum of retrospective and prospective strategies in a two-

Table 2. Spectrum of retrospective and prospective strategic options

	Opportunities from failure	
Responses to failure	**Reality improving:** Opportunity occurs in the same value chain in which the failure occurs.	**Goal creating:** Opportunity occurs in a value chain other than the one in which failure occurs.
Reality tuning: A changeable or controllable reality is tuned to the existing goal level.	**Retrospective** Find and correct the causes of failure	
Goal adapting: The goal is adapted to the unchangeable or uncontrollable reality.	**Prospective** Explore news ways to use failure	

dimensional matrix using the two factors discussed above.

Because the retrospective approach to failure is to find and correct the causes of failure, the upper left area—where tuning and improving reality appears—represents the retrospective approach best. On the other hand, because the prospective approach to failure is to explore new ways to use failure, the lower right area—adapting and creating goals—represents the prospective approach best. However, the line between the two approaches might not be dichotomous but rather continuous, which is why the two approaches are visualized as the opposite ends of a spectrum.

Four Strategic Options for Dealing with Failure

Such a continuous distinction between the retrospective and prospective strategies can be specified with four discrete strategic options. Table 3 lists how the combinations of the two dimensions yield four different strategic options for dealing with failure. It should be noted again that the line between each of four strategic options is not always clear. The strategic options suggested in this study are instead 'archetypes' that may be used in a mixed form in practice. Each of the four strategic options listed in Table 3 is explained using widely known examples.

Table 3 Four strategic options for dealing with failure

Responses to failure	Opportunities from failure	
	Reality improving: Opportunity occurs in the same value chain in which the failure occurs.	**Goal creating:** Opportunity occurs in a value chain other than the one in which failure occurs.
Reality tuning: A changeable or controllable reality is tuned to the existing goal level.	**Spurring:** use the apparent failure as the impetus to overcome a deep-seated problem	**Outflanking:** achieve the aimed reality indirectly by pursuing a new goal
Goal adapting: The goal is adapted to the unchangeable or uncontrollable reality.	**Revaluing:** accept the unwanted and irreversible reality, but make the most of the hidden values accompanied by the reality	**Re-anchoring:** accept the unwanted and irreversible reality, but explore new goals in which failure can be a seed

Spurring

The upper left area of Table 3 represents the *spurring* strategy—the combination of *reality tuning* and *reality improving*. This strategy involves using an apparent failure as an impetus to overcome a deep—seated problem at hand. How did the United States use the USSR's threat in the space race? In 1962, seven years before Apollo

11's successful moon landing, President John F. Kennedy delivered a famous speech in which he said "We choose to go to the moon··· not because they are easy, but because they are hard, because that goal will serve to organize and measure the best of our energies and skills..." Collins and Porras, in their best seller *Built to Last: Successful Habits of Visionary Companies*, pointed to this tactic by suggesting the concept of BHAG (i.e., Big Hairy Audacious Goals), which is an excess goal that can help prompt more efficiency and innovation. As many industrial experts have noted, what makes Samsung unique and competitive is a consistent 'sense of crisis' for constant vigilance and innovation. In 1988, the American Red Cross (ARC) had much problem revealed by an FDA inspection related to technology assets for a blood service. However, the ARC reformed its blood operations far beyond FDA requests by using the poor state of the blood service as an impetus to envision revolutionizing the service.

Revaluing

The lower left area of the table represents *revaluing* strategy—the combination of *goal adapting* and *reality improving*. This strategy involves accepting the unwanted and irreversible reality but also making the most of the hidden values accompanied by the reality. For instance, this strategy is incorporated into the so-called 'last-mover advantage,' which refers to the last mover who lost a lead in market having an advantage to learn from the first mover's trial and error. Therefore, rather than trying to defeat the first mover, the last mover may focus more on learning from the first mover by remaining the last mover. As another example, the revaluing strategy was behind the birth of Post-it note. When scientist Spencer Silver at the 3M Company invented a new adhesive in 1968, he found that it was not so strong enough to hold paper on a surface. However, another scientist, Art Fry, found that the weak adhesive was very useful to mark books because it did not leave any residue even after being used several times. *Revaluing* is also found in an urban management case, High Line, the famous landmark in New York City. Instead of demolishing the abandoned railroad track, the city rejuvenated it as a new public park beneficial for children's education, local economic opportunities, and community building.

Outflanking

The upper right area of the table represents the *outflanking* strategy—the combination of *reality tuning* and *goal creating*. This strategy is to achieve the aimed reality indirectly by pursuing a new goal. In the concept of 'judo management,' which refers to the martial art judo, a competitor's excess momentum or investment can be reversely used as his or her inertia. The essence of this strategy is to focus on achieving a goal not by sticking to the traditional and direct manner but by employing new innovative and indirect ways. In medicine, vaccines are another example of outflanking. Deliberately imitated infections (i.e., vaccines) are used to enhance immunity. In two classic books on military strategies, *36 Ancient Chinese Strategies* and *Art of War*, the authors recommended not engaging in a head-to-head contest against an enemy but instead using an enemy's inertia or over-commitment (i.e., using an appearance of a deficiency to make the enemy feel overconfident or complacent, which can result in the enemy being defeated eventually).

Re-anchoring

The lower right area of the table represents *re-anchoring* strategy— the combination of *goal adapting* and *goal creating*. This strategy is to accept the unwanted and irreversible reality, but to explore new goals in which failure can be a seed for new success. During WWII, the United States and the United Kingdom realized that the USSR would be a new threat to them. But rather than confronting this threat, President Roosevelt and Prime Minister Churchill decided to collaborate with Stalin in order to achieve other goals (i.e., defeating another common enemy, the Nazis). As for Apple, Steve

Jobs' death in 2011 was an unavoidable loss. However, Apple successfully ensured that Steve's death eclipsed the problems of the iPhone 4S that had been much criticized prior to Steve's death. Oxfam America (OA) suffered a public relations setback due to Oxfam Quebec's financial scandal in 1992. However, in the wake of the scandal, OA recreated its 'brand' value by banding its eight affiliates together not only to protect themselves from the aftermath of Quebec scandal, but also to achieve a new goal: build a stronger Oxfam International with a more expanded mission.

Q2. HOW CAN WE ASSESS HOW WELL WE ARE PREPARED TO USE FAILURE?

Beyond the strategic options of failure management noted above, the second question—*How can we assess how well we are prepared to use failure?* —will be answered in this section. Simply put, the preparedness of failure management is the capability to learn and make constructive decisions in the face of failure. The details of the learning mechanism surrounding failure follow below.

Five Common Stages for Learning through Failure

As discussed above, failure management is an attempt to learn from failure retrospectively and prospectively. Failure management means that failure can and should be analyzed deliberately in order to gain new knowledge pertaining to the causes of failure and pursue new opportunities beyond the current mental model. In a nutshell, failure management is a learning process through failure. With the learning process of failure management in mind, answering the second question may necessitate a review of learning and decision -making processes for failure management. First, reviewing prior studies related to learning and knowledge creation reveals five common stages of learning through failure.

- Preparing stage: The decision maker is aware of fallible event or the benefit of failure before failure can significantly influence his or her organization.
- Reflecting stage: The decision maker recognizes and applies his or her awareness of benefit of failure to (the anticipated or unanticipated) failure, thereby devising strategic option to facilitate the benefits of failure.
- Monitoring stage: The decision maker monitors and recognizes (the anticipated or unanticipated) failure as it actually occurs.
- Facilitating stage: The decision maker implements prepared strategic options or improvises new strategic options to

benefit from failure.

- Memorizing stage: The decision maker records new knowledge about the fallible event and the benefit of failure, implicitly or explicitly.

It should be noted that the five common stages outlined above are implemented not in a linear process, but rather in different permutations. The permutation of the five learning stages can vary according to two factors.

Factor One: Do We Anticipate Failure in Advance?

The first factor that determines the learning process through failure management is the answer to the question "Do we anticipate failure in advance?" This question pertains to whether certain fallible events (or the possibility/symptom/signal of failure) are anticipated before the failure is actually monitored (i.e., before the actual failure has a significant influence on the organization). Therefore, as for any fallible event, there are two possibilities: 1) the failure is anticipated (i.e., precedent or remembered); or 2) the failure is unanticipated (i.e., unprecedented, or precedent but forgotten).

Factor Two: Are We Aware of the Benefit of Failure in Advance?

The second factor influencing the learning process through failure management is the answer to the question "Are we aware of benefit of failure in advance?" This question pertains to whether the decision maker is aware of the benefits of fallible event before the failure is actually monitored (i.e., before the actual failure has a significant influence on the organization). A decision maker can be aware of the benefit of failure through firsthand experience or secondhand learning such as best practices of management, axiom, norms, proverbs, or any other historical knowledge of management. Accordingly, there are also two possibilities for the decision maker: 1) he or she is aware of the benefit of failure in advance; or 2) he or she is unaware of the benefit of failure in advance.

Three Types of Preparedness of Failure Management

The two factors noted above determine how the five common stages of learning are combined and sequenced. As a result of such dynamics, there are three different types of permutations that can be referred to as three types of preparedness of failure management (FM): *planned FM*, *prepared FM*, and *improvised FM* (see Table 4 and Fig. 1).

Table 4 Three types of preparedness of failure management

Are we aware of the benefits of failure in advance?	Do we anticipate failure in advance?	
	Anticipated	Unanticipated
Aware	**Planned FM** (Using foresight)	**Prepared FM** (Using foresight & hindsight)
Unaware	**Improvised FM** (Using hindsight)	

Planned FM: Using Foresight

In *planned FM*, the decision maker anticipates failure and recognizes the benefit(s) of the failure before the failure is actually monitored. Therefore, the decision makers' attitude toward failure can be phrased as follows: "We are ready to use anticipated failure, which is a good bet. So, we actively utilize it (even wait for or look for failure, or intentionally fail)." With this attitude, the failure at hand is not a failure any more. Instead, it is a good option to consider. In other words, the (avoidable or unavoidable) failure at hand can be countenanced or even fostered as long as the failure can add new significant value or benefits.

Apple's tactic in the face of Steve Jobs' death in 2011 is an example of *planned FM*. Apple had anticipated Steve's death but could not avert it. Instead, Apple planned to strategically commemorate his death, which successfully discouraged the criticisms against the newly released iPhone 4S. Apple saw its sales

Figure 1. Three types of preparedness of failure management

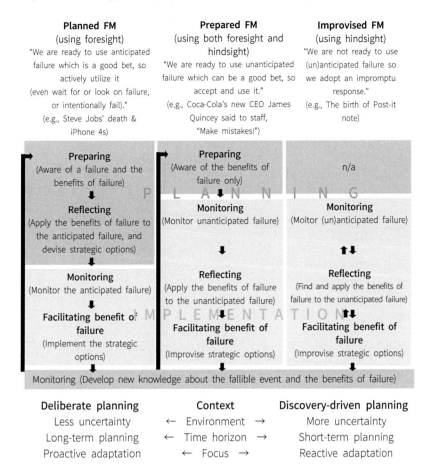

Planned FM (using foresight) "We are ready to use anticipated failure which is a good bet, so actively utilize it (even wait for or look on failure, or intentionally fail)." (e.g., Steve Jobs' death & iPhone 4s)	Prepared FM (using both foresight and hindsight) "We are ready to use unanticipated failure which can be a good bet, so accept and use it." (e.g., Coca-Cola's new CEO James Quincey said to staff, "Make mistakes!")	Improvised FM (using hindsight) "We are not ready to use (un)anticipated failure so we adopt an impromptu response." (e.g., The birth of Post-it note)
Preparing (Aware of a failure and the benefits of failure) ↓	**Preparing** (Aware of the benefits of failure only) ↓	n/a
Reflecting (Apply the benefits of failure to the anticipated failure, and devise strategic options) ↓	**Monitoring** (Monitor unanticipated failure) ↓	**Monitoring** (Moitor (un)anticipated failure) ↑↓
Monitoring (Monitor the anticipated failure) ↓	**Reflecting** (Apply the benefits of failure to the unanticipated failure) ↓↑	**Reflecting** (Find and apply the benefits of failure to the unanticipated failure) ↑↓
Facilitating benefit of failure (Implement the strategic options) ↓	**Facilitating benefit of failure** (Improvise strategic options) ↓	**Facilitating benefit of failure** (Improvise strategic options) ↓

Monitoring (Develop new knowledge about the fallible event and the benefits of failure)

Deliberate planning	Context	Discovery-driven planning
Less uncertainty	← Environment →	More uncertainty
Long-term planning	← Time horizon →	Short-term planning
Proactive adaptation	← Focus →	Reactive adaptation

explode after Jobs' death because customers began to see iPhone 4S as the last legacy of Steve Jobs.

In general, for *planned FM*, the learning stages of failure management are combined in this order: Preparing (aware of a failure and the benefits of failure) → Reflecting (apply the benefits of failure to the anticipated failure, and devise strategic options) →

Monitoring (monitor the anticipated failure) → Facilitating (implement the strategic options devised in advance) → Memorizing (record new knowledge about the fallible event and the benefits of failure, implicitly or explicitly).

Prepared FM: Using Both Foresight and Hindsight

In *prepared FM*, the decision maker does not anticipate failure in advance but instead knows the benefit of the failure even before the failure is actually monitored because he or she already knows the best practices of management that have been used for similar failures in the past. Therefore, the decision maker's attitude toward failure can be phrased: "We are ready to use unanticipated failure, which can be a good bet. So we accept and use it." In a nutshell, the decision maker uses foresight from secondhand learning, but at the same time he or she also uses hindsight that can be earned while applying secondhand knowledge to the unanticipated failure after it occurs.

Upon taking office in 2017, Coca-Cola's new CEO James Quincey said to his staff "Make mistakes!" He pointed to the lack of innovation as deriving from the company's over-cautiousness. His message was to foster new experiments in terms of products, management and business models, even if they were highly risky. Quincey may not know what kinds of mistakes or failures will occur in the future. However, he certainly has a willingness and even the confidence to positively use the outcome of any failure in the process of new experiments because he already knows failure can be beneficial.

Therefore, in *prepared FM* the learning stages of failure management are combined in this order: Preparing (aware of the benefits of failure only) → Monitoring (monitor unanticipated failure) → Reflecting (apply the benefits of failure to the unanticipated failure) → Facilitating (improvise strategic options to facilitate the benefits of failure) → Memorizing (record new knowledge about the fallible event and the benefits of failure, implicitly or explicitly).

Improvised FM: Using Hindsight

In improvised FM, regardless of whether the failure is anticipated or not, the decision maker does not know the benefit of the failure before the failure is actually monitored. Therefore, the attitude of the decision maker toward failure can be phrased: "We are not ready to use (anticipated or unanticipated) failure, so we adopt an impromptu response." In short, improvised FM is a case of "learning by doing" through trial and error. In fact, improvised FM is the origin of all failure management because every lesson originates from firsthand experience. In other words, after a firsthand experience, new knowledge learned from the firsthand learning is shared by others in the form of secondhand knowledge (e.g., best practices of management).

The birth of Post-it note is an example of *improvised FM*. The inventor created a new cohesive which was not as strong as he thought. But later another scientist recognized the value of such weak cohesive that can be used to mark books without leaving residue on the surface of paper. The Post-it note represents not only a creation of new product but also a revaluation of the product. In this case, neither failure nor the benefits of failure were known in advance. However, the failure was used beneficially through the improvised recognition of the benefits of failure.

In *improvised FM*, the learning stages of failure management are combined in this order: Monitoring (monitor anticipated or unanticipated failure) → Reflecting (find and apply the benefits of failure to the failure) → Facilitating (improvise strategic options to facilitate the benefit of failure) → Memorizing (record new knowledge about the fallible event and the benefits of failure, implicitly or explicitly).

Contexts in Which the Three Types of Preparedness are Used

Fig. 1 summarizes not only the logical flows of the three types of preparedness of failure management but also the various contexts where the three types of preparedness are used or needed in terms of the environment, time horizon, and focus in response to failure.

First, *planned FM* is used when the decision maker is already prepared with knowledge about the beneficial use of failure—this situation is close to *deliberate planning*. In other words, *planned FM* can be more often used in cases of less uncertainty, in long-term planning, and for proactive adaptation to one's environment. On the other hand, *improvised FM* involves relying on impromptu activities without any knowledge of failure management; it is similar to *discovery-driven planning*, which is more appropriate in cases of more uncertainty, in short-term planning, and for reactively adapting to one's environment. Lastly, *prepared FM* has the characteristics of both *planned FM* and *improvised FM*, and its contextual position of is between that of *deliberate planning* and *discovery-driven planning*.

Which type of preparedness is superior to the others? The answer can vary. However, what is certain is that the appropriateness of each type of preparedness depends on the environmental context. In other words, because each of the three types of preparedness has its own advantages depending on the certainty of the environment and the time horizon of the planning, it would be desirable for any organization to be ready to use any of the three types of preparedness to fit any situation.

"My power is made perfect in weakness." 2 Corinthians 12:9

Failures can be beneficially used by an organization. However, developing creative strategies in the face of failure is easier said than done. The difficulty of enacting good strategies is partially attributed to tunnel vision in the face of failure. The more imperative a failure is, the more nearsighted we can be. How can we get over such bounded rationality when failures and challenges confront us? In order to help answer this question, this study has suggested that the following two ideas can complement the present framework of failure management.

First, this study examined how failures can benefit every corner of management, regardless of where the management failure occurs. In detail, there are four strategic options—*spurring, revaluing, outflanking,* and *re-anchoring*—through which we can diversify the diffusion of benefits of failure throughout an organization. Such findings practically imply that the awareness of the four strategic options can help decision makers more methodically consider both retrospective and prospective strategies when faced with failures and challenges.

Second, such strategic options can be planned, prepared, and improvised through various mechanisms depending on an organization's (or decision maker's) preparedness. Some organizations that practice *planned FM* would have sufficient foresight to anticipate failures and prepare strategies to use the failures in advance. Other organizations or individuals practicing *improvised FM* would not have such foresight; they would instead rely on hindsight to determine improvised strategies to benefit from failure after it occur. And some other organizations employing *prepared FM* would have the characteristics of both *planned FM* and *improvised FM*.

In summary, failures can be beneficial as long as they can be re-assessed and utilized retrospectively or prospectively through creative strategies. Furthermore, the process of such re-assessment and utilization of failures can vary according to how well decision makers or organizations are prepared to use failure in a certain contexts (e.g., environmental certainty and time horizon).

Noteworthy is the fact that the models presented in this paper are only the archetypes, i.e., the basic elements of organizational strategies. In practice, the four strategic options of failure management and the three types of preparedness are used in any combinations.

SELECTED BIBLIOGRAPHY

For the original idea of failure management, see: Lee, J., & Miesing, P. (2017). How Entrepreneurs Can Benefit from Failure Management. *Organizational Dynamics*, 46(3), 157−164. http://dx.doi.org/10.1016/j.orgdyn.2017.03.001.

For the *value chain, see: Porter, M. (1985). Competitive Advantage.* Free Press.

For grounded theory, see: Glaser, B. G., & Strauss, A. L. (1967). *The Discovery of Grounded Theory: Strategies for Qualitative Research.* Chicago: Aldine; Eisenhardt, K. M. (1989). Building Theories from Case Study Research. *Academy of Management Review*, 14(4), 532−550.

For BHAG, see: Collins, J. & Porras, J. I. (1994). *Built to Last: Successful Habits of Visionary Companies.* New York: Harper Business.

For the 'judo management,' see: Yoffie, D., & Cusumano, M. (1999). Judo Strategy: The Competitive Dynamics of Internet Time. *Harvard Business Review*, 77(1), 70−81.

For learning processes, see: Ackoff, R. (1989). From Data to Wisdom. *Journal of Applied Systems Analysis*, 16, 3−9; Nonaka, I. (1991). The knowledge creating company. *Harvard Business*

Review, 69(6 Nov−Dec), 96−104; Kolb, D. (1984). *Experiential Learning: experience as the source of learning and development.* New Jersey: Prentice−Hall; McGrath, R. G. & MacMillan, I. C. (1995). Discovery−Driven Planning. *Harvard Business Review*, 73(4), 44−54; Miller, W. L. & Morris, L. (1999). *Fourth generation R&D: managing knowledge, technology, and innovation.* John Wiley & Sons, Inc.

For deliberate planning and discovery−driven planning, see: McGrath, R. G. & MacMillan, I. C. (1995). Discovery−Driven Planning. *Harvard Business Review*, 73(4), 44−54.

CHAPTER 03 Success management*
: Dynamic sustainability beyond
harms of success

Junesoo Lee, Seung-Joo Lee

SUCCESS, AN IMPEDIMENT TO SUSTAINABLE MANAGEMENT

SUCCESS STRIKES BACK! Why do businesses fail? Paradoxically, one of the major causes of business failure is prior experience with success. Given that the working definition of success is 'a state where reality is superior to the goal,' many management scholars and practitioners assert that success, ranging from trivial emotional satisfaction or an enemy's fall to great sales performance, can be harmful to sustainable management. Success often fosters over-confidence, complacency, and biases in decision-making and investment. Success can tarnish the uniqueness of an organization's

---

* To cite the original manuscript of this chapter, use this reference: Lee, J., & Lee, S.-J. (2018). Success Management: Dynamic Sustainability beyond Harms of Success. *Organizational Dynamics*, 47(4), 209–218.
https://doi.org/10.1016/j.orgdyn.2018.09.004.

products and services and harm its relationships with other players in the market ecosystem. What drives this 'winner's curse' or 'resource curse'? How can we successfully deal with the negative aspects of success? Toward answering these questions, we employed a grounded theory approach — based on an extensive review of the existing literature and case studies — to explore the paradoxical impacts of success. From these analyses, we developed the success management (SM) framework, which helps us to systematically recognize and avoid the pitfalls and negative consequences of success.

HARMS OF SUCCESS I: INTERNAL DECISION-MAKING BIAS

Success can be detrimental to both the internal and external sides of an organization. These negative outcomes of success may occur simultaneously, both before and after success is achieved. Table 1 presents a comprehensive list of the negative effects of success and the different contexts and stakeholders involved in each pitfall.

Table 1 Harms of success

Internal decision-making bias due to success			
Initial		Cognition	Over-confidence
			Anchoring
		Aiming	Over-aiming
			Complacency
		Reasoning, attribution	False positive (no effect, but winner thinks there is)
			False negative (adverse effect, but winner thinks not)
Consequential		Internal network	Conflict over credit or excess resources
			Rigid coalition resisting change
		Investment bias (Table 2)	Deficient investment
			Excess investment
External backfire due to success			
Reactive		Customers	Flooding, draining customers
			Isolated, satiated customers; base effect
		Intermediaries (suppliers, partners)	Withdrawn support
			Lost ecosystem
		The general public	Flattery
			Nitpicking
Aggressive		Adversaries (regulators, competitors)	Exposed weakness
			Revenge, depredation
			Chicken game, arms race

Cognition

Overconfidence Success can foster and reinforce over-confidence, which can lead to biased decision-making. When we are overconfident, we tend to be overly optimistic and overestimate our strengths and capabilities. Nokia at its peak in 2007 was the global leader in the mobile-phone industry and one of the world's most valuable brands. Trapped by its past success, the company overestimated its capabilities in software and failed to deliver smartphones that met customers' expectation. Management saw the shift from hardware to software, but the organization was dominated by hardware engineers who underestimated the importance of software and lacked the capabilities to develop user-friendly operating systems and apps.

Anchoring Success can reinforce psychological and institutional inertia. Continuously achieving success and frequently sharing success stories can anchor the status quo within an organization. Anchoring can include path-dependence, inertia, mental delay, tunnel vision, resistance to reform, etc. Eventually, anchoring reinforces the magnitude and longevity of an existing bias so that the conventional way of thinking or acting is maintained regardless of relevant environmental changes. In short, when we are too absorbed by or committed to any one success (or success factor), we can become buried by it and, therefore, blind to the trade-off between the bright and dark sides of the success. Even though Kodak created the world's first digital camera, the company failed to make the transition to digital technology and fell behind the Japanese. Kodak managers viewed digital camera as a threat to its highly profitable film business, and resisted change and adaptation. Kodak failed to reinvent itself as habitual ways of thinking like the razor-and-blade model was deeply anchored in the mindset of managers.

Aiming

When success occurs, it can lead to a bias in goal setting, which can result in over-aiming or complacency.

Over-aiming   Success commonly encourages a level of self-confidence that motivates people to aim higher. However, when confidence reaches a certain point, it can inspire commitment to unachievable goals. As a result of this 'Icarus paradox' (i.e., aiming for the unachievable), the sustainability of internal resources is often ignored. This causes the overuse, enervation, and depletion of these internal resources. In 2006, Toshiba surprised the world when it announced the acquisition of Westinghouse's nuclear power business for $5.4 billion USD. Despite its lack of experience in the nuclear power business, Toshiba desperately needed a new growth engine. Top management was highly optimistic about its future and decided to go ahead with this make or break deal. However, the market collapsed after the Fukushima nuclear disaster in 2011, as governments around the world stopped new investments and strengthened regulations. This unforeseen shift forced Toshiba to write down more than $6.3 billion USD in 2017 and sell its highly profitable semiconductor business.

Complacency   In contrast to over-aiming, success can also cause organizations to reduce efforts and lower goals. Organizations can lose their sense of purpose and entrepreneurial spirit and may develop rigidities and routines that inhibit adaptation and innovation. This 'eroding goals' phenomenon, when caused by success, often occurs not only in mature, well-performing businesses but also in startups that celebrate prematurely. The decline or depression witnessed after success may result from exhaustion, a sense of relief, or simple carelessness. Firms caught in the success trap need to reestablish a healthy balance between exploitation of their current activities and exploration of new ones.

Reasoning, Attribution

In addition to aiming, another type of bias can be caused by success-induced overconfidence and anchoring. Success can lead people to misinterpret the relationships between certain management tools and goals. Overconfidence and anchoring can cloud judgment; both factors contribute to the inability to appropriately select goals and the management tools best-suited to achieve them.

False positive (Type I error)   False positives are basically conceptually identical to Type I errors in inferential statistics. Even when there is no actual relationship between two things (e.g., goal and tool), success-induced overconfidence can make us believe that there is a positive relationship. These false notions can be aggravated by our tendency to attribute success to endogenous or controllable causes (e.g., internal strategies and skills) even when the true causes are exogenous and uncontrollable (e.g., economic boom, downfall of a competitor). A tactic that is successful today is not guaranteed to be successful tomorrow due to changes in the external environment. For example, the formula for Walmart's success in the US may not be applicable to other countries. The presumption that customers, competitors, suppliers, and labor unions in other countries behave similarly to those in the US was proven wrong by Walmart's painful withdrawal of its stores from Germany and South Korea.

False negative (Type II error)   Conversely, when two things are negatively related, success-induced overconfidence can blind us to this adverse association. This phenomenon is referred to as Type II error in statistics. Type II errors are made partially because we ignore the fact that information is delivered with delays in the system. When we do not pay attention to the long-term consequences of actions influenced by overconfidence, we become prone to nearsighted decision-making. For example, Apple employs Samsung to supply the semiconductors required to manufacture the iPhone. Because Apple was dependent on Samsung as a long-term supplier of critical components, Apple revealed its supply chain management strategies and practices to Samsung. As a result, Samsung was able to learn from Apple and then implement their management strategies, thus becoming a strong competitor for Apple. In short, Apple's short-term success with its supplier exposed the company to detrimental con-sequences and threats to their long-term success.

When Type I and Type II errors occur simultaneously during decision-making, we may mistakenly perceive a positive relation-ship between two things that are actually negatively related. This situation is often observed in developing countries. For example, since the 1990s, China has experienced an increase in income level that has been accompanied by a decrease in the overall health of its citizens. This likely occurred because the Chinese people started consuming more junk food while paying less attention to the adverse effects on their health. Sadly, this harmful pattern has not changed over time because they still incorrectly infer a positive relationship between income and health when the two are actually indirectly negatively associated.

Internal Network

Internal conflict over credit or excess resources Success

can aggravate internal conflict over the credit for the success or the use of excess resources. For example, many lottery winners experience misfortunate relationships with their friends and family due to controversies on how to spend their fortunes. Additionally, the recent Volkswagen emissions scandal was largely attributed to internal conflicts amongst management, which compromised their integrity and led to a massive economic loss. In sum, extra resources or opportunities due to success can make multiple internal interests compete with one another and thereby distort preferences or priorities in decision making.

Rigid coalition resisting change On the contrary to (or as a result of) the internal conflict due to success, success may also make people unite against change. Success is often followed by groupthink or 'sunflower management' where team members tend to comply with their leaders. Internal stakeholders who have earned success together tend to form tighter bonds than existed before the success. Such a tightly coupled internal network makes it harder for individuals to modify their behavior, lest it induce changes harmful to their ingrained interests. Sony's great success in the 1980s and 1990s helped many specialized departments con-struct fiefdoms. This departmentalization became an impediment toward growing the unity needed to develop an online digital music service. This internal fragmentation eventually undermined the company's leadership in the global electronics industry.

Investment

All of these internal biases and conflicts result in biased investments. An abnormal or imbalanced investment represents the biased and abused attention, powers, and resources; this eventually produces a biased investment portfolio that does not fit the environment. For example, excessive investment in a successful product may cause the firm to invest deficiently in other products, thereby jeopardizing their healthy portfolio of products. Table 2 details these two types of investment biases.

Deficient investment One type of investment bias, deficient investment, manifests itself as complacency, sticking to the successful design of an organization, herd mentality or groupthink, sluggishness, under-focusing on the target market, positioning narrower than the market niche, and outdated quality behind market needs. Well-known declining companies including Kodak, Nokia, Wang, and Blackberry all engaged in such investment biases.

Excess investment Excess investment functions conversely to deficient investment. Apple's LISA in 1983, Sony's LED TV in

Table 2. Investment bias in detail

Object of investment			Bias of investment (i.e., false distribution of attention, power, and resources)	
			Deficient	Excess
Organization	Organization orientation	Objectives	Complacent	Over-aiming
		Organization design (structure, process, HR, incentives)	Sticking to the successful design	Keeping unnecessary restructuring
	Decision-making	Direction	Herd effect, groupthink	Conflict over credit or excess resources
		Pace	Sluggish, rigid	Speeding, hasty, wild
Market	Market, customers	Target	Under-focus on the mark	Over-focus off the mark
		Diversification	Narrower than niche	Wider than niche, overstepping
	Products, services	Quantity	Deficient	Redundant
		Quality	Outdated behind market needs	Too radical beyond market needs
Examples			• Kodak • Nokia • Wang • Blackberry	• Apple's LISA in 1983 • Sony LED TV in 2004 • PDA before smartphone • Chrysler's failed business diversification in the mid-1980s

2004, and the personal digital assistant (PDA) before the era of smartphones represent exemplary cases of excessive investment. Those products were born out of accelerated decision-making that failed to fully consider the market maturity. As a result, those products exhibited excess quality and required price points that were incompatible with their market environment. When it comes to quantity, overconfidence often leads to overproduction which leaves price slump. And another example: Having been fascinated by the great successes under the legendary leadership of Lee Iacocca, Chrysler continued to diversify its businesses into the aviation industry and sports car manufacturing in the mid-1980s. However, this diversification turned out to be a waste of money because the investment was not based on rigorous market analyses but rather on the successful leader's personal desires. Excess investment is also found in human resource management. Although the so-called 'performance-based reward system' has proven successful in the private and public sectors, an excessive focus on external rewards for performances may drive away motivation that seeks internal or mental rewards.

In practice, deficient and excessive investments often exist simultaneously during biased decision-making. For instance, the declining performance of Sears is attributed to both deficient and excessive investment. During the early 1990s, Sears made a deficient investment in business innovation by ignoring a new trend, driven by Walmart, which provided new services to customers beyond the conventional shopping experience. On the other hand, Sears made excessive investments in financial businesses that were distant from its core competitiveness in the 1990s. Sears was overly optimistic in their forecasting of the aging customers' financial needs when, in actuality, the new and original businesses were not as synergistic as expected.

HARMS OF SUCCESS II: EXTERNAL BACKFIRE

Customers

Flooding customers   After a success garners popularity among customers, the consumer demand and corresponding responsibilities are likely to increase to unmanageable levels. This 'customer service' can eventually deteriorate the quality of the product or service.

Draining customers   Customer flooding can give rise to two negative consequences. First, it can drive away historically steady customers that become dissatisfied with the deteriorating services. Additionally, the 'crowding-out effect' of a successful attraction may cause native residents to leave due to cost increases unaffordable to them; this is called gentrification when rent hikes affect urban planning. Second, the rush of customers is most likely just a flash in the pan. When these new fickle customers move on, the business is usually left with excess inventory.

Isolated customers   Biased marketing on a successful product can isolate potential customers. For example, sales of North Face's winter jacket have exploded among South Korean teenagers over the past few years. But, since North Face's marketing has only focused on its currently successful market segment (i.e., teenagers), the company has isolated potential adults customers, leaving them reluctant to buy North Face products.

Satiated customers A success may make the subsequent fair or good performance look bad or worse in comparison, which is called 'base effect' through which internal or external observers may have an inflated expectation of my performance. Furthermore, even the longevity of a product or service can satiate customers. Let us again use North Face as an example. Although North Face's winter jacket had a unique competitiveness in terms of price and quality, sales declined considerably when North Face lost customers who got bored with the 'old uniqueness' of North Face and attracted by other brands that had since caught up with North Face's technology.

Intermediaries (suppliers, partners)

Withdrawn support Upon certifying a person's or a company's success, external supporters may feel that they are no longer needed and cut back on their support. The primary issue with this seemingly reasonable reaction to the company's success is that supporters are making their decision to withdraw based on the appearance of the company's success and not based on the company's actual need for continued support.

Lost ecosystem Most enterprises want to win in competition by enervating or even driving competitors out of the market. However, competitors usually play multiple roles, not only as opponents but also as partners. The presence of competitors can be beneficial because they push businesses to improve and help foster greater attention and demand from customers through a cluster effect. Therefore, a complete annihilation of competitors through successive victories may actually shrink a company's market. The decline of once thriving companies (e.g., Polaroid, Wang Laboratories) exemplifies the fatal outcome of the stand-alone strategy.

The General Public

Flattery Those who want to take advantage of a company's success can try to win favor with the company by giving positive and favorable news. This biased information can impair judgment and eventually reinforce an organization's internal bias.

Nitpicking Fame and popularity can generate nitpicking from external stakeholders. Even without any direct gain, others may disparage high-achieving people or companies simply out of jealousy or a desire for reciprocity; for example, the many 'anti-fans' of pop and sports stars.

Adversaries (regulators, competitors)

Exposed weakness Fame helps reveal weakness by drawing more attention to the details. Korean pop singer Psy's revolutionary hit song 'Gangnam Style' in 2012 made him surprisingly popular worldwide. But, this popularity also exposed that he had sung an anti-American song that disparaged the US troops deployed in South Korea. Quickly responding to the incident, he released a sincere apology to the press in the hopes of swaying American public opinion to become less adverse and even sympathetic to him.

Revenge Revenge from an opponent or loser is the most anticipated byproduct of success. In contrast to nitpickers, those who seek revenge have a considerable conflicting interest. For example, the fierce competition in the smartphone market sparked a legal battle in 2012 between Samsung and Apple, with each company trying to harm the other's success.

Depredation Excess resources earned through success can generate internal friction over a certain stakeholder's resources and also cause external stakeholders to desire depredation of the resources. These external stakeholders extend beyond just com-petitors to include everyone that recognizes the success. Lottery winners are often overwhelmed with strangers who request generous donations and attempt to extort their newfound wealth.

Chicken game, arms race The worst-case scenario caused by the adverse outcomes of success is probably counter-productive competition among successful competitors. The desire to outdo competitors may produce self-destructive results through excessive competition. In this case, compromise or collaboration for co-prosperity is not considered to be an option.

How can we address and resolve the various negative impacts of success? Primarily, of course, we must recognize the existence of the problem. The specific actions required may vary according to factors such as the characteristics of the problem, decision-makers' interpretations of the problem, levels of strategies and tactics, etc. Some remedial measures are presented below toward resolving the harms of success.

TOWARD REMEDYING THE HARMS OF SUCCESS

"Freedom is not free." An American saying engraved into a wall at the Korean War Veterans Memorial, Washington, D.C.

Success may cost risks. Further, sustainable success should cost sacrifices. In 2014, there were two memorable events relevant to SM. First, CVS stopped selling cigarettes because the stable source of profit from cigarettes did not correspond to the company's mission to contribute to public health. In the same year, Tesla, Inc. decided to open and share their patents with their competitors. It was a counter-intuitive but insightful strategic decision that demonstrated Tesla's confidence and their willingness to foster the ecosystem of the electronic car industry. How can we promote this forward-looking strategy rather than being nearsighted and buried by today's success? How can we pursue dynamic sustainability rather than the naïve and static sustainability driven by the disadvantages of success? How can we prevent the harms of success prophylactically or at least correct them afterward? There are many diverse studies that address the harmful aspects of success in the literature. Some keywords repeatedly recommended to overcome the pitfalls of success are presented in Table 3.

Organization-based Objectives of SM

To overcome the negative effects of success, an organization must maintain internal and external sustainability by assuring who they are, whom to serve, how to serve, and when to proceed or stop. Internally, decision-makers should maintain grounded confidence free of illusions and biases. Externally, firms should maintain the unique value of their products and services in order to sustainably co-exist in the market ecosystem. But how are these achieved? The keywords that inform the process of maintaining the soundness of internal decision-making and external positioning, even in the face of success, can be divided into adjectives and nouns that relate to an organization's management, as described below.

NOUNS of Organization-based Management
: Strategy and Validation (S&V)

The 'nouns' of management relate to the kind of activities within an organization involved in strategy and validation (S&V). Toward sustainable management, strategies are made and validated in a three-dimensional fashion. First, S&V decisions are based on values, beliefs, data, information, benchmarks, and other reference points. Second, S&V decisions are processed within an organization through systems that encompass value chains, decision-making processes, governance structures, communication channels, financing, reward systems, human resources, capacity, technology, assets, motives, mindset, ethics, norms, culture, leadership, internal and external controls, monitoring, and evaluation. Third, S&V are discussed and addressed to interact with external objects such as customers, market niche, intermediaries (e.g., suppliers, partners), the general public, and adversaries (e.g., regulators, competitors).

ADJECTIVES of Organization-based Management : Characteristics/Directions of S&V

The success of the S&V nouns in management depends on how they are managed. This 'how' can be described by 'adjective' keywords that are commonly found in academic and practical recommendations for SM as listed below.

Mission-oriented The design of products or services is based on the core values of an organization. However, once a product becomes successful among customers, it easily takes priority and often replaces the core values, thereby makes us susceptible to the influence of market fads. A successful product makes the organization focus only on whether they are going their way rightly, while ignoring whether they are going the right way. Products or services should be invented, designed, and revisited in terms of how they fulfill the core mission and values of the company. But what kind of mission? The exemplary missions of sustainable companies usually contain the values of helping, serving, contributing to, and sharing with people. Sony serves as a positive example of the benefits of having a mission-oriented company. Since the 1950s, Sony had committed itself to the mission,

'To experience the sheer joy of innovation and the application of technology for the benefit and pleasure of the general public.' The value Sony cherished was a reliable guide that helped the company introduce successful creative products (e.g., transistor radio, MiniDisc, and Walkman) for a long period of time. In short, Sony's success in relative terms (i.e., first in electronics) resulted from the company's focus on absolute value.

Genuine Toward grounded decision–making, data and information should be exchanged openly and transparently within an organization. This type of communication is possible only when those involved are humble (i.e., realizing their limitations through self–reflection, feeling self–sufficient, and grateful to helpers' credits) so that they can reach a correct attribution, share empathy, and pursue harmonious relations. The founder of Costco, Jim Sinegal, institutionalized an exemplary internal control. His policy was to cap margins to no more than 15%, not only to maintain price competitiveness in the wholesale market but also to keep the company from greed. In another example, since 2014, two children have died after being crushed by IKEA dressers. However, the multinational furniture retailer's responses to the incidents have been delayed, irresponsible, and inconsistent across different countries, which has significantly affected the company's image. As Jim Collins argued in his book 'Good to Great,' modesty is a common characteristic of leaders of sustainable organizations. Modest leaders are more rational, grounded, and tend to attribute success to external factors and failure to themselves.

Simple Decision-making is often distorted due to excessive information, rather than a lack of information. Simplification of strategy and communication helps prune less important elements in order to focus on the more crucial elements. This is needed because organizations have certain capacities that may limit the number of elements on which they can focus. Also, considering the limited cognitive capacity of humans, communication needs to be clear and concise rather than prolonged and discursive. President John F. Kennedy's 'landing a man on the Moon' initiative might be one of the most shining examples of this concise but very compelling communication strategy.

Objective Successful leaders are tempted to wield more power based on their past successes. Regardless of whether the success came from one capable person, information source, or management structure, depending on a single component that has provided excellence in the past may lead an organization to a risky future. However, being down-to-earth is not easy because success encourages bias and over-confidence. How can we make S&V objective, fair, dispassionate, and rigorous? Using counter-weights, such as listening to opposing or seemingly redundant information and using decentralized communication channels, often helps to keep our thinking grounded, balanced, complementary, and versatile. Famous leaders in history have often used such tactics. For example, Winston Churchill recognized both the bright and dark sides of his charismatic leadership, so he established an independent statistical office that was designed to provide an objective and rigorous analysis of the situation. Another way of remaining objective is taking a break to rest and becoming detached from the work, which prevent us from becoming too absorbed in our current path. Bill Gates, in order to rest and reflect, used to have "think weeks" completely secluded from his family, friends, and even Microsoft.

New   In a rapidly changing environment, progressive adaptation might be the only way to achieve sustainability. The goal of progressive adaptation is to keep alert and vigilant by questioning the status quo and exploring and experimenting with the unknown. Many successful sustainable organizations (e.g., Procter & Gamble, 3M, Hewlett-Packard) focus on "continuous improvement." They know that their values and missions are unattainable, but instead, serve as inspiration for continuous improvement.

Repeated The reform or innovation of an organization is not a single event, but a long process. Revising the status quo and exploring the unknown need to be constant, continual, and persistent efforts. At the same time, these efforts need to be systematic and institutionalized so that even a major change of leadership or governance will not destabilize the innovation. Adidas's balanced and institutionalized efforts have continued since the inception of their sustainability strategy in 1989. The impact of this consistency was confirmed by their ranking as one of the 'Global 100 Most Sustainable Corporations in the World' in 2014. Another virtue of repetition lies in the limitation of our intelligent capacity. Because of the limited time and resources dedicated to decision-making, we often rely on intuition or inevitably guess. If we have to resort to such heuristics often, in reality, we need to educate and train our intuition and guesses repeatedly until making reasonable decisions becomes an instinctive part of our skillset.

Multi-staged In a highly unstable environment, the formula for today's success will need to be tested again tomorrow. Such experiments necessitate a multi-staged approach that employs gradual, incremental, and diversified trials and modifications. When other companies launched online drugstores driven by the dot-com fever in the late 1990s, Walgreens just waited to benefit from the late-movers' advantage. After embarking on the first stage, which involved a long but prudent contemplation on the new trend, Walgreens advanced to the second stage by designing a sophisticated online service. Walgreens.com, which was launched as the third stage, turned out to be more successful than other drugstores that developed their Internet sites prior to Walgreens'.

Holistic   If we could fully appreciate the life cycle of our systems or products in advance, or if we could foresee the outcome of today's actions, no one would make a hasty or nearsighted decision. Adverse success occurs when today's success begets tomorrow's failure. According to the basic principles of economics, many restaurants increase their prices after customer flow increases. Price hikes may temporarily cause greater cash inflow, but can eventually result in the loss of steady customers due to negative word-of-mouth. What we will face tomorrow is the result of what we do today, which is all the more because (1) we are living in a network where all actors' activities are intertwined and influencing one another and (2) the results of our actions come out not immediately but often over time. By keeping this delayed feedback loop in mind, our decisions can become more patient, prepared, far-sighted, and holistic. Setting aside during the boom years for a rainy day or emergency fund is another good example of being well-prepared and far-sighted. Since the early 1990s, Texas has been operating the economic stabilization fund (ESF), which was designed to save tax revenues and prepare for a rainy day due to oil price fluctuation and economic recession. As of 2017, Texas seems to be well-overcoming this 'resource curse' because it has the nation's largest ESF and effectively uses it for economic stabilization.

Paradoxical   We often learn more from failure than from success. No matter how well we manage our organizations, we may encounter failures, from trivial to fatal. If failure is hard to fully prevent and somewhat inevitable, the second best alternative is to learn from the experiences of failure. The concept of failure management (FM) is a new perspective that serves to illuminate and utilize the paradoxical benefits of failure. Initially, 3M regarded the Post-it note as a failure because it was not as adhesive as expected. Later, 3M revaluated the Post-it note and found that its adhesive was strong enough to mark books repeatedly and then placed it on the market where customers found the new need for a weakly adhesive note. Essentially, FM dictates that failure can be used as a seed for success. In contrast to FM, SM focuses on the dark side of success. In order to realize the so-called 'planful opportunism' in a turbulent environment, the two paradoxical ideas of FM and SM need to be implemented as a part of effective strategic planning.

Yin-Yang (dilemma-embracing) Even though we keep the suggestions mentioned above in mind, there are still hard dilemmas when trying to remedy the harms of success. For instance, decentralized decision-making may either be a condition for an objective strategy or a seed for chaotic management. Also, experimental investments may either bring new opportunities or eclipse the organization's potential. However, SM is more successful when we struggle to recognize and resolve dilemmas than when we become stubborn due to success. Furthermore, one of the obstacles of sound decision-making in such dilemmas is dichotomous thinking, such as good vs. bad, forceful vs. empowering, strategic vs. operational, centralized vs. decentralized, etc. This linguistic and conceptual dichotomy may endanger realistic thinking because strategic options are often continuous (e.g., volume dial) rather than dichotomous (e.g., on/off switch). Dichotomous approaches lead to the false notion that different options, which may be compatible in reality, are mutually exclusive or incompatible. Therefore, continuous and compatible thinking, which the widely known Yin-Yang diagram represents, may help embrace and resolve dilemma during S&V. The authors of the book 'Fear Your Strength' introduced the relevant example of Sandy Koufax, the Los Angeles Dodgers fastball-throwing pitcher who was having difficulty choosing between slow and fastball throws. His perfect game in 1965 was the result of his continuous and compatible approach because he threw 'the right pitch (i.e., fastballs, curveballs, change-ups) in the right situation.'

Table 3. Remedies for the harms of success

Organization-based management toward success management (SM)

ADJECTIVES: Characteristics and directions of S&V	NOUNS: Strategy and validation (S&V)	SM objectives

Mission-oriented
Value-oriented (accountable, responsible, helping, serving, contributing, sharing, sacrificing), rather than profit-/product-/ranking-oriented
Genuine
Open, transparent, honest, clean, righteous
Humble, modest, self-reflecting, knowing limit
Self-sufficient, grateful
Listening, empathic, harmonious, collaborative
Simple
Clear, concise
Focused, determined
Objective
Detached, dispassionate, fair, selfless
Rigorous, grounded, down-to-earth
Counter-weighted, kept in check, balanced
Complementary, redundant, decentralized
Grouped, team-based
New
Innovative, exploring, experimental, learning
Questioning, alert, vigilant, non-stop
Repeated
Constant, continual, regular, persistent
Contemplating
Trained, disciplined, institutionalized, systematic
Multi-staged
Gradual, incremental, diversified
Holistic
Far-sighted, big-picture, patient
Preparing, provident, saving
Networked thinking, feedback-loop/systems thinking
Paradoxical
Failure-management perspective
Success-management perspective
Yin-Yang (dilemma-embracing)
Continuous (not 'on/off switch' but 'volume dial')
Compatible (not 'versus' but 'with')
	Ground of S&V
	Values, beliefs
	Data, information
	Benchmark, reference
	
	Internal objects of S&V
	Value chain
	Decision-making process
	Governance structure
	Communication channels
	Financing
	Reward system
	Human resource, capacity
	Technology, assets
	Motives, mindset
	Ethics, norms, culture
	Leadership
	Internal/external control
	Monitoring, evaluation
	
	External objects of S&V
	Customers, market niche
	Intermediaries (suppliers, partners)
	The general public
	Adversaries (regulators, competitors)
		Pursuing dynamic sustainability by keeping assuring …
		  Who we are,
		  Whom to serve,
		  How to serve, and
		  When to go or stop
		
		Internally, having grounded confidence and pride
		
		Externally, maintaining the uniqueness of products and services for co-existence in the market ecosystem

"If you think you are standing firm,

be careful that you don't fall."

1 Corinthians 10:12

For organizations that continue to thrive today, the fact that they have been successful is indisputable. However, the efficacy of the strategies behind their past successes may change with the ever-changing environment. Therefore, in an instable environment, the stability of being is sustained only through the dynamics of doing.

Success is something all organizations pursue but today's success can be the seed of tomorrow's failure because success makes us prone to bias and backfire. How can we recognize and overcome the harms of success? The answer may lie, ironically, in FM. Different from other management tools that help avert adversity, such as risk management (RM) or crisis management (CM), the essence of FM is to utilize failure by identifying and embracing its potential benefits. Like FM, adversity should also be recognized and cherished during SM (Fig. 1). In other words, sustainable S&V in an organization requires that we forgo the monopoly on power and resources that can be earned from success. The key to the door of sustainable success is to control

Figure 1 Failure management and success management toward dynamic sustainability

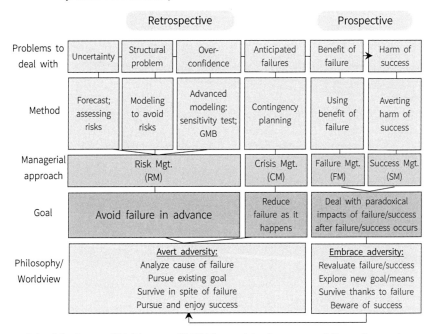

	Retrospective			Prospective		
Problems to deal with	Uncertainty	Structural problem	Over-confidence	Anticipated failures	Benefit of failure	Harm of success
Method	Forecast; assessing risks	Modeling to avoid risks	Advanced modeling: sensitivity test; GMB	Contingency planning	Using benefit of failure	Averting harm of success
Managerial approach	Risk Mgt. (RM)			Crisis Mgt. (CM)	Failure Mgt. (FM)	Success Mgt. (SM)
Goal	Avoid failure in advance			Reduce failure as it happens	Deal with paradoxical impacts of failure/success after failure/success occurs	
Philosophy/ Worldview	Avert adversity: Analyze cause of failure Pursue existing goal Survive in spite of failure Pursue and enjoy success			Embrace adversity: Revaluate failure/success Explore new goal/means Survive thanks to failure Beware of success		

Before failure/success: RM & CM can use FM & SM framework to discover any variables worth managing

After failure/success: Once a new variable is discovered through FM & SM, it can be managed by RM & CM

Source: Adapted from Lee, J. & Miesing, P. (2017). How Entrepreneurs Can Benefit from Failure Management. *Organizational Dynamics*, 46(3), 157−164.

(or even limit) resources, freedom, or strengths by sticking to the mission and value for which the resources are given (or should be used). In doing so, the resources, freedom, or strengths are less likely to be an impediment to internally grounded decision-making, nor a stimulus for external backfire.

In sum, the SM framework provides retrospective and pro-spective answers to the question "Why did we succeed?" If you answer, "We succeeded due to (or because of) a certain past cause," you are taking a retrospective view on success and focus on the grounded attribution of success. And if you think, "We succeeded due to (or for) a certain future purpose," your view is prospective and mission–oriented.

The frameworks introduced in this paper comprehensively include both drivers of negative impacts of success and remedies to these problems. However, they may not be exhaustive enough to cover every issue of SM. Some of the conceivable challenges we need to keep addressing include (1) how the drivers behind the harms of success may have different impacts based on the characteristics of the specific success (e.g., the type, magnitude, duration, and phase of success), and (2) how we can design and implement targeted remedial strategies to effectively manage each type of success' many pitfalls.

SELECTED BIBLIOGRAPHY

For the operational definition of success and failure, and the failure management (FM), see: Lee, J., & Miesing, P. (2017). How Entrepreneurs Can Benefit from Failure Management. *Organizational Dynamics*, 46(3), 157−164. https://doi.org/10.1016/j.orgdyn.2017.03.001; Lee, J. (2018). Making Hindsight Foresight: Strategies and Preparedness of Failure Management. *Organizational Dynamics*, 47(3), 165−173. https://doi.org/10.1016/j.orgdyn.2017.12.002.

For the comprehensive list of decision−making biases such as overconfidence or anchoring, see: Bazerman, M. H., & Moore, D. A. (2008). *Judgment in Managerial Decision−making* (7th ed.). Wiley.

For the comprehensive study of overconfidence, see: Müller, A. (2007). *Impact of Overoptimism and Overconfidence on Economic Behavior: Literature Review, Measurement Methods and Empirical Evidence*. Diplomarbeiten Agentur diplom.de.

For the paradoxical relationship between wealth and health in China, see: Du, S., Mroz, T. A., Zhai, F., & Popkin, B. M. (2004). Rapid income growth adversely affects diet quality in China−particularly for the poor! *Social Science & Medicine*, 59, 1505−1515.

For the Sony case and other failed success cases, see: Herbold, R. J. (2007). Seduced by Success: *How the Best Companies Survive the 9 Traps of Winning*. McGraw-Hill.

For the 'grounded confidence,' see: Hayward, M. (2007). *Ego Check: Why Executive Hubris is Wrecking Companies and Careers and How to Avoid the Trap*. Kaplan Business.

For the modest leadership, Winston Churchill, Walgreens, Boeing and IBM cases, see: Collins, J. (2007). *Good to Great*. HarperCollins Publishers.

For the 'continuous improvement' and 'planful opportunism,' see: Collins, J., & Porras, J. (1997). *Built to Last*. HarperCollins Publishers.

For the 'networked thinking,' see: Barabasi, A. (2003). *Linked: How Everything is Connected to Everything Else and What It Means for Business, Science, and Everyday life*. Plume.

For the 'feedback-loop thinking' and 'systems thinking,' see: Meadows, D. H. (2008). *Thinking in Systems*. Chelsea Green.

For the 'Yin-Yang' approach and Sandy Koufax case, see: Kaplan, R. E., & Kaiser, R. B. (2013). *Fear Your Strengths: what you are best at could be your biggest problem*. Berrett-Koehler Publishers, Inc.

CHAPTER 04

Balanced SWOT*
: Revisiting SWOT analysis through
failure management and
success management

Junesoo Lee, Seung-Joo Lee, Kwon Jung

REVISITING SWOT ANALYSIS

One of the most popular and widely used frameworks in strategic
management is SWOT analysis (or SWOT hereafter), which represents
the analysis of 'strengths, weaknesses, opportunities, and threats.'
SWOT helps identify the positive and negative factors in the
external and internal environment of an organization. The primary
goal of SWOT is to conduct a situation analysis in order to identify
the key issues, problems, or challenges facing the organization and
to develop insights into the strategic direction of the organization.

---

* To cite the original manuscript of this chapter, use this reference: Lee, J., Lee,
  S.-J., & Jung, K. (2020). Balanced SWOT: Revisiting SWOT Analysis through
  Failure Management and Success Management. *KDI School Working Paper Series*,
  20−17.

SWOT has become widely accepted not only in the business and private sector but also in the public and non-profit sectors, such as the government, schools, hospitals, NGOs, and international organizations. The framework provides a synthesis and logical structure that is clear, objective, comprehensive, and relatively easy to implement.

However, the simplicity of SWOT can be a double-edged sword. While praising the convenience of SWOT thanks to its simplicity, SWOT users have also criticized the oversimplified results and processes included in SWOT analyses. In today's dynamic and rapidly changing environment, the strengths of an organization can become weaknesses, while a threat can become an opportunity.

Table 1 Conventional SWOT analysis

Organizational environment	Impact on organizational objectives	
	Beneficial	Harmful
Internal	Strengths	Weaknesses
External	Opportunities	Threats

As seen in Table 1, the conventional SWOT analysis is conducted using a two-by-two matrix consisting of two dimensions—organizational environment (i.e., internal and external) and impacts of the environment on the organizational objectives (i.e., beneficial and harmful). As a result of the interaction of the two dimensions, the table presents four ingredients for analyses and strategies–strengths, weaknesses, opportunities, and threats. However, analysts and practitioners can often be frustrated by the blurry line between strengths and weaknesses as well as between opportunities and threats. In the turbulent environment within and outside an organization, yesterday's strength can be today's weakness and vice versa. Likewise, today's threat can be tomorrow's opportunity and vice versa.

In short, when one is using conventional SWOT analysis, the common sense of management is often challenged by two questions: Are strengths or opportunities always beneficial? Are weaknesses or threats always harmful? By answering these questions, this article examines the paradoxical faces of organizational environments, both theoretically and practically, to suggest a refined version of SWOT analysis that can embrace these paradoxes.

FAILURE MANAGEMENT & SUCCESS MANAGEMENT

Before diving into refining SWOT, it is necessary to understand the methods used to analyze and deal with the ambivalent impacts of organizational environments. Recently, a new managerial perspective has been materialized in the form of two management tools—failure management (FM) and success management (SM). The spirit and content of FM and SM may not be new, but they provide a new perspective through which we can more systematically face and interpret the paradoxes of management.

Failure Management (FM)

In the framework of failure management, failure is operationally defined as 'a state where reality is inferior to the goal or expectation.' According to this definition, failure means not only bankruptcy or total loss but also any state in which we feel em-barrassed or disheartened — for instance, conflict, disappointment, frustration, regret, and, especially, weaknesses and threats in terms of SWOT analysis. The core idea of failure management is about how to systematically recognize and use the bright side of failure. Therefore, the operational definition of failure management is 'systematic ways to use the benefits of failure.' The framework of FM comprises three sub-methods — propositions, strategies, and preparedness, as covered below.

FM Propositions

The first method of FM consists of sixteen propositions, each of which represents a unique way of using failure beneficially. The sixteen propositions are the products of the interaction of three types of failure (deficiency, excess, and inconsistency) and six purposes for using failure (learning, saving, reforming, discouraging, attracting, and complementing). Each of the sixteen proposition can be summarized as: (1) *learning new knowledge*, (2) *re-using deficiency*, (3) *saving surplus for superior opportunity*, (4) *conserving resources and spreading risk*, (5) *improving effectiveness and efficiency*, (6) *stimulating innovation*, (7) *challenging status quo and averting bias*, (8) *reducing risk or threat*, (9) *deepening opponent's inertia or over-commitment*, (10) *discouraging threat through instability*, (11) *inducing external help*, (12) *drawing attention or meeting new demands*, (13) *stimulating or vitalizing support*, (14) *getting and nurturing complementary forces*, (15) *checking, eclipsing, or uniting against threat*, and (16) *offsetting another inconsistency with opposite pattern*. How these propositions are applied in actual business cases will be presented in the following sections.

FM Strategies

Although the sixteen propositions of FM comprehensively specify the benefits of failure, there is a need for simplified guidelines that can help deal with failure more conveniently. With this in mind, the methods of using failure can be categorized into four strategic options of FM. First, *spurring* is to use the apparent failure as the impetus to overcome a deep-seated problem. Second, *revaluing* is to accept the unwanted and irreversible reality while making the most of the hidden values accompanied by the failed reality. Third, *outflanking* is to indirectly achieve the aimed−for reality by pursuing a new goal. Fourth, *re−anchoring* is to accept the unwanted and irreversible reality while exploring new goals for which failure can be a seed.

FM Preparedness

The third method of FM is concerned with how well an organization is prepared to handle failure beneficially. Considering two factors (if failure is anticipated in advance and if the benefit behind failure is known in advance), three types of FM preparedness are conceivable. First, *planned FM* is an organizational state in which an organization is ready to use anticipated failure that can be a good opportunity, so the failure is actively utilized, i.e., failure is waited for, looked on, or even intentionally created. Second, *prepared FM* is a state in which an organization is ready to use unanticipated failure that can be a good opportunity, so the unanticipated failure is willingly accepted and used. Third, *improvised FM* is a state in which an organization is not ready to use anticipated or unanticipated failure, so the failure is dealt with by an impromptu response.

Success Management (SM)

In contrast to FM, success management focuses on the dark side of success. The operational definition of success is 'a state where reality is superior to the goal or expectation.' Based on this definition, success represents not only an objectively achieved goal but also any subjective feeling of achievement—for example, satisfaction, relief, contentment, and strengths and opportunities in the SWOT context. Similar to FM, the gist of success management is about how to recognize and avert the dark side of success. Therefore, the operational definition of SM is 'systematic ways to avert the harms of success.' The framework of SM also consists of three sub-methods—propositions, strategies, and preparedness, as follows.

SM Propositions

First, nineteen propositions represent the negative impacts of success. Among the nineteen, the first ten propositions are about the harmful impacts of success on internal decision-making: (1) *over-confidence*; (2) *anchoring*; (3) *over-aiming*; (4) *complacency*; (5) *false positive* (i.e., winner thinks that his action has a positive effect even though the action is not the real cause of success); (6) *false negative* (i.e., winner thinks that his action has no effect even though the action has an adverse effect in the long run); (7) *conflict over credit or excess resources*; (8) *rigid coalition resisting change*; (9) *deficient investment*; and (10) *excess investment*. The remaining nine propositions are about the harmful impacts of success on external relationships: (11) *flooding, draining customers*; (12) *isolated, satiated customers (base effect)*; (13) *withdrawn support*; (14) *lost ecosystem*; (15) *flattery*; (16) *nitpicking*; (17) *exposed weakness*; (18) *revenge, depredation*; and (19) *chicken game, arms race*.

SM Strategies

The SM framework also suggests a set of remedies for the adverse effects of success. The remedial strategies of SM consist of ten categories that are expressed as adjectives: (1) *mission-oriented* (focusing more on the core value responsible for service, rather than on nearsighted tangible returns); (2) *genuine* (staying open and humble); (3) *simple* (keeping communication messages clear and focused); (4) *objective* (being rigorous, checked, and balanced); (5) *new* (maintaining a challenging status quo and innovating); (6) *repeated* (normalizing and institutionalizing something that is beneficial); (7) *multi-staged* (taking an incremental and multi-phased approach); (8) *holistic* (considering the big picture and pursuing systems thinking); (9) *paradoxical* (considering the counter-intuitive impacts of success and failure); and (10) *Yin-Yang* (taking a continuous perspective rather than a discrete one, and having a compatible perspective rather than a dichotomous one).

SM Preparedness

The third method of SM is about how well an organization is prepared to handle the negative impacts of success. Similar to FM, the SM framework suggests three types of SM preparedness. First, *planned SM* is an organizational state in which an organization is ready to handle the anticipated negative impact of success, so the success is proactively dealt with. Second, *prepared SM* is a state in which an organization is ready to manage unanticipated success that can have a negative effect, so the unanticipated success is handled readily and wisely. Third, *improvised SM* is a state in which an organization is not ready to manage anticipated or unanticipated success, so the adverse impact of success is dealt with only after it is experienced.

In summary, the frameworks of FM and SM provide the lens through which we can systematically recognize and analyze the paradoxical impacts of failure and success. How these methods of FM and SM can help in improving SWOT will be presented in the following sections.

As discussed earlier, the conventional SWOT analysis does not specify how to recognize and deal with the two paradoxes: the bright side of failure (i.e., weaknesses or threats) and the dark side of success (i.e., strengths or opportunities). To reflect the two kinds of paradoxes in SWOT, the existing SWOT table must be altered. First, the original dimension of 'impact' must be renamed 'primary impact.' Next, a new dimension of 'secondary impact' must be added to the SWOT table. The secondary impact has the same categories as the primary impact: beneficial and harmful.

As shown in Table 2, the new SWOT analysis table is different from the original one because it contains the dimension 'secondary impact.' As a result of the additional dimension, the four original features of SWOT (i.e., strengths, weaknesses, opportunities, and threats) are divided into eight features, with each feature of S.W.O.T. re-categorized into 'beneficial' and 'harmful' elements. The original four features of SWOT are renamed to emphasize the initial meanings (i.e., strengths → beneficial strengths; weaknesses → harmful weaknesses; opportunities → beneficial opportunities; threats → harmful impacts), while the four new features (highlighted in Table 2) stress the paradoxical impacts of each of the features of S.W.O.T. (i.e., harmful strengths, beneficial weaknesses, harmful opportunities, and beneficial threats). In the following sections, the ways of achieving a balanced SWOT analysis through FM and SM are presented in detail.

Table 2. Balanced SWOT analysis with the additional "secondary impact" dimension

Organizational environment	Primary impact		Beneficial
	Beneficial	Harmful	Harmful
Internal	Beneficial strengths	Beneficial weaknesses	Harmful
External	Harmful strengths / Harmful opportunities	Harmful weaknesses / Harmful threats	Secondary impact
	Beneficial opportunities	Beneficial threats	Harmful
			Beneficial

Dealing with the Positive Impacts of Failure

The first paradox of management— the bright side of failure—is highlighted in Table 3. Today's internal weaknesses or external threats (i.e., primary impacts) can be transformed into tomorrow's strengths or opportunities (i.e., secondary impacts), though such transformations are not made immediately. The bright side of weaknesses or threats should be analyzed and recognized first; then the beneficial weaknesses can be regarded as part of strengths, while the beneficial threats can be considered as part of opportunities, as described in Table 3. Below are four cases that show how the new SWOT embracing FM can help find beneficial weaknesses and threats hidden behind failures.

Table 3. Balanced SWOT analysis through failure management

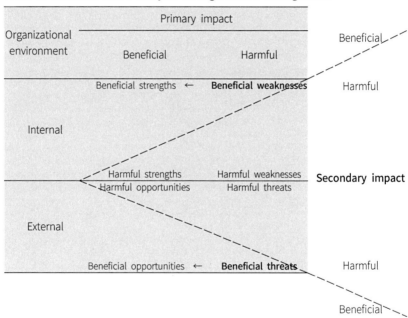

Case 1: iPhone 4S

When the iPhone 4S was launched on the market as a successor to the iPhone 4 in 2011, Apple fans were disappointed by the new product's innovation, which was far from their expectations. The criticism of the iPhone 4S coincided with the death of the legendary CEO of Apple, Steve Jobs. His death seemed imminent, and therefore it signified the loss of Apple's greatest internal asset. However, Jobs left Apple with another chance to regenerate the iPhone 4S. Immediately after his demise, sales of the iPhone 4S exploded because Apple made the iPhone the last legacy of Steve Jobs; people were eager to possess their hero's last breath. The case represents how an avoidable loss of an internal asset can actually help reduce external threats through a series of pre-determined plans.

FM Proposition From the perspective of conventional SWOT, the loss of Steve Jobs should be considered a weakness of Apple. With FM applied to SWOT, however, Apple can find that its legendary boss, through his demise, left a new opportunity of *reducing risk or threat.*

FM Strategy Apple could not prevent Jobs' death. In facing such an unavoidable loss, the best thing Apple could do was finding another way to make the loss beneficial. In other words, Apple used the *re-anchoring* strategy, through which it found a new goal in promoting iPhone 4S sales after (and also thanks to) Jobs' passing.

FM Preparedness Long before his death, Apple knew that its boss's health was deteriorating and that the loss was inevitable. Such prior knowledge helped Apple prepare for responses to the tragic event as well as the tragedy itself; this can be called *planned FM.*

Case 2: Post-it Notes

In 1968, 3M encountered a setback when a 3M expert discovered an adhesive that was much weaker than intended. Not until years later did a colleague of this expert suggest using the weak adhesive as part of a new product that could satisfy customers' new needs for sticky notes. This resulted in the creation of Post-it Notes. In this case, an invention of deficient quality was re-valued to attract new demands through a hindsight-based strategy.

FM Proposition The original output of 3M research was just another failure, which is usually a part of the organization's weakness. However, 3M carried out the failure management method of *re-using deficiency*, through which the weak adhesive was re-used as a new product later.

FM Strategy　3M did not attempt to change or correct the failure by making a stronger adhesive. Instead, it employed the *revaluing* strategy by discovering a hidden value of the weakness and thereby released a revolutionary product: Post-it Notes.

FM Preparedness　The failure of the original research was not fully anticipated. The beneficial impact of the weak adhesive was not within the mental model in 3M. Not until long after the failure did the company discover the new value of the failed project. That is why this case can be called *improvised FM*.

Case 3: Space Race

Although an American—Neil Armstrong—stepped on the Moon for the first time in 1969, it was a Russian—Yuri Gagarin—who, in 1961, became the first human to travel to space. There was a fail-ure management in the US between the two historic events—land-ing on the Moon and orbiting the Earth. After the US was outrun several times by the successful Russian space projects, in 1962 President John F. Kennedy delivered a famous public speech at Rice University: "We choose to go to the moon in this decade and do the other things not because they are easy, but because they are hard, because that goal will serve to organize and measure the best of our energies and skills." Thanks to the Russian threat in the Space Race, the US government earned national (including Congressional) support for the space program and invested an exorbitant amount of resources into the Apollo program. The result is the history that we well know. When facing an unprecedented threat, the US used it as an opportunity to spur and stimulate technological and managerial innovations.

FM Proposition Confronted with the Soviet Union's threat, the US leadership decided to use the lost Space Race as a chance for *stimulating innovation* nationwide. Almost all US citizens supported President Kennedy's national aim and Congress did not cut back on the budget proposed by NASA by even one dollar. The technological breakthroughs generated by the Apollo program could not have been achieved without the initial threat posed by the USSR.

FM Strategy The threatening news of Russia's feat in space exploration was a great shock to the US people. Accompanied by the growing threat of nuclear weapons in the 1960s, the loss in the Space Race aggravated the shock and also helped the US employ the *spurring* strategy to stimulate innovations in almost all social domains.

FM Preparedness   Although the astounding performance of the Russian cosmonauts was threatening to the US, it was not as surprising to the US government officials who had previously experienced innumerous crises throughout US history. Rather, these historical lessons taught them how to utilize such a crisis to mobilize the entire nation into a desired state. Therefore, the US's eventual victory in the Space Race can be attributed to the *prepared FM.*

Case 4: Judo Management

What distinguishes judo from other martial arts, such as boxing and taekwondo, is the fact that judo players try to win not by directly hitting or punching but, rather, by indirectly using their opponents' inertia—that is, a heavier opponent has more inertia and, therefore, would be easier to trip over one's leg. Such 'judo management' is a strategy to reversely use external threats as an opportunity to indirectly calm them down.

FM Proposition   Transforming an opponent's strength into his weakness is an FM attempt of *deepening opponent's inertia or over-commitment.* Like 'David and Goliath,' big corporations have large-scale organizations and systems, which can conversely present them with failure in the form of being unable to quickly respond to the market environment. Meanwhile, small companies with lean and efficient systems may win the competition in the market due to their better celerity and adaptability.

FM Strategy　Instead of directly confronting a big and powerful opponent, we can use the FM strategy of *outflanking*, i.e., trying to win indirectly simply by having our opponent overdo himself in the game so that he cannot move flexibly, which will eventually cause him to fall.

FM Preparedness　Regardless of whether or not we know that we will encounter a powerful opponent in advance, and also regardless of whether or not we know that the opponent's power can be used reversely beforehand, we can employ the inertia of that opponent as long as we are quick and wise enough to adopt the outflanking strategy. Therefore, judo management may be applicable in any FM preparedness effort.

The aforementioned cases of failure management are sum-marized in Table 4. The table shows how the negative features (i.e., weaknesses and threats) of conventional SWOT are revalued as beneficial weaknesses and threats through the balanced SWOT using the FM approach.

Table 4 Cases of failure management in the balanced SWOT

Cases		iPhone 4S	Post-it Note	Space race	Judo management
Conventional SWOT		Weakness	Weakness	Threat	Threat
Failure management	Proposition (Benefits of failure)	Reducing risk or threat	Re-using deficiency	Stimulating innovation	Deepening opponent's inertia or over-commitment
	Strategy	Re-anchoring	Revaluing	Spurring	Outflanking
	Preparedness	Planned FM	Improvised FM	Prepared FM	Any type of preparedness
Balanced SWOT		Beneficial weaknesses		Beneficial threats	

SUCCESS MANAGEMENT & BALANCED SWOT ANALYSIS

Dealing with the Negative Impacts of Success

Table 5 highlights the second paradox of management (i.e., the dark side of success). Internal strengths or external opportunities that exist today can lead us to new troubles tomorrow. As described in Table 5, the harmful strengths and opportunities can be analyzed and re-identified as weaknesses and threats, respectively. Following are four cases that show how the new SWOT incorporating SM can help in finding and dealing with harmful strengths and oppor-tunities behind success.

Table 5 Balanced SWOT analysis through success management

Organizational environment	Primary impact		Beneficial
	Beneficial	Harmful	Harmful
Internal	Beneficial strengths	Beneficial weaknesses	
	Harmful strengths → Harmful weaknesses		Secondary impact
	Harmful opportunities → Harmful threats		
External			Harmful
	Beneficial opportunities	Beneficial threats	Beneficial

Case 1: CVS

In 2015, CVS, a nationwide convenience store chain in the US, declared that it would no longer carry cigarette products. This must have been a tough decision, as cigarette sales accounted for a large proportion of the company's entire revenues. However, relying on profits from harmful products may have actually tarnished the company's aims and appearance. Therefore, after a long period of soul-searching, CVS decided to put an end to the negative impact that selling harmful items had on the company's mission and sustainability.

SM Proposition CVS found that its strength in harmful item sales could blind the company and lead it to *over-aiming*. Success in sales could make the company overcommit itself to pursuing profits only, which may eventually result in declining value inside and outside the company.

SM Strategy The SM strategy that CVS employed was to be *mission-oriented*. Tangible sales performance may overshadow intangible assets such as human-centric services and social values. CVS chose to be not just an enviable company but also a respectful one.

SM Preparedness For a long period throughout the company's history, CVS had carried cigarette products. However, the decision to ban these products in stores was made only after the company valued the negative effects of such sales. Therefore, CVS carried out an *improvised SM* because it had made the decision long after the negative effect of its cigarette sales had occurred.

Case 2: Tesla

In the same year, 2015, Tesla, Inc., the pioneering company in the electric car industry, announced that the company would begin opening and sharing its own patents for electric car technology so that any company can use them. The cost of the decision was evident, as the company's valuable internal assets were about to be shared with others. However, the benefit of opening patents had to be evaluated from a more holistic perspective. As electric cars are fueled electrically, the success of an individual electric car manufacturer depends heavily on the whole industry's co-prosperity, which will result in the creation of a large number of electricity charging stations. In other words, Tesla needed two things: the predominant use of electric cars and the prevalence of electricity charging stations. To expand and secure the 'eco-system' of the new industry, Tesla decided to willingly bear the short-term costs in exchange for the long-term benefits.

SM Proposition What led Tesla to the counter-intuitive decision to open patents was the company's fear of a *lost ecosystem* in the electric car market. No matter how strong the company is, and no matter how good its cars are, those cars cannot run on the street if there are no charging stations—and such stations will become available only when the electric car market has expanded to a sufficient level. Therefore, to survive in the future, Tesla had to rescue its competitors in the present by sacrificing the company's strengths—i.e., patents—as intellectual assets.

SM Strategy Tesla's decision was possible because of the long-term perspective that enabled the company to predict that a small sacrifice today would beget a big result tomorrow. Such a long-term sense of causation was Tesla's SM strategy of having a *holistic* view.

SM Preparedness   Like all other private companies that depend on uncertain and sensitive market situations, Tesla had to be prudent in deciding to open its patents. The costs and benefits of such a decision were assessed through a predetermined plan, which was a *planned SM*.

Case 3: Costco

Since its inception, Costco has adhered to its unique price policy, which controls the sales margin under a certain level, e.g., 15%. One of the greatest concerns of Costco founder Jim Sinegal was that the big opportunities in the market would beget harmful avarice inside the company and thereby negatively impact the business's sustainability. Therefore, the rationale behind the control of market opportunity and profits was the founder's belief that a minimum level of prices would not only benefit customers but also prevent the company from being greedy.

SM Proposition   Costco's anticipated market opportunity could have backfired, as a great profit could have blinded the company and resulted in *over-aiming*. Therefore, the founder knew not only when to move but also when to stop; he wanted to avoid the adverse effects of market opportunity.

SM Strategy   The SM strategy that Costco employed was to be *genuine*. Costco's founder kept listening to his inner voice so as to humble himself and become self-sufficient, which helped him carefully setting a limit of business.

SM Preparedness   Costco wisely foresaw the negative impact of market opportunity, and also the need for limiting profits. Such precognition resulted in *planned SM* that helped protect the company from harm caused by profit opportunities.

Case 4: Winston Churchill

One of the great leaders during WWII, Winston Churchill, knew that he was strong-willed, as well as a genius. What made him greater was that he knew that the favorable environment surrounding his genius could be a seed for his over-confidence, which could ruin everything. Therefore, he determined that he needed a new environment which can help control himself so that he could remain objective. Eventually Churchill directed the cabinet to open the Central Statistical Office (CSO) whose major function was to provide him and other governmental staff with proven and objective information based in reality. In doing so, Churchill prevented the positive environment inside and outside himself from becoming negative in the long run.

SM Proposition   Churchill found that his opportunity, i.e., the external support and praise of his power and intelligence, could lead to *overconfidence* and *anchor* the methods he used in the past. The negative rigidity stemming from his success could have led to failure, which he wanted to avoid.

SM Strategy   The SM strategy that Churchill used was to stay *objective*. Among the various strategies that he could use to keep himself objective, he ended up relying on external control. That external force was the scientific and rigorous analysis provided by the statistics office, which allowed Churchill to remain unbiased.

SM Preparedness   As is widely known, Winston Churchill was not always successful throughout his career. He experienced many failures in and out of battle. However, the wisdom that he acquired through his failures prepared him to be a great leader who could control himself during his days as prime minister; this was Winston Churchill's *prepared SM.*

Table 6 summarizes the four cases mentioned in this section. It shows how the features that have been considered as positive in conventional SWOT analyses (i.e., strengths and opportunities) can be re−assessed as harmful strengths and opportunities through a new SWOT analysis balanced through success management.

Table 6 Cases of success management in the balanced SWOT

Cases		CVS	Tesla	Costco	Winston Churchill
Conventional SWOT		Strength	Strength	Opportunity	Opportunity
Success management	Proposition (Harms of success)	Over-aiming	Lost ecosystem	Over-aiming	Overconfidence, anchoring
	Strategy	Mission-oriented	Holistic	Genuine	Objective
	Preparedness	Improvised SM	Planned SM	Planned SM	Prepared SM
Balanced SWOT		Harmful strengths		Harmful opportunities	

BALANCED SWOT ANALYSIS FOR WINDOW OF OPPORTUNITY

When the four paradoxical features—beneficial weaknesses, beneficial threats, harmful strengths and harmful opportunities—are re-positioned in the SWOT table, the refined SWOT table would appear as Table 7, which can be called 'balanced SWOT.' The table contains the positive and negative sides of the conventional four S.W.O.T. features.

Table 7 Balanced SWOT Analysis

Organizational environment	Impact on organizational objectives	
	Positive	Negative
Internal	Beneficial strengths Beneficial weaknesses	Harmful strengths Harmful weaknesses
External	Beneficial opportunities Beneficial threats	Harmful opportunities Harmful threats

Organizational management is full of paradoxes. Under the paradoxical dynamics of management, the achievement of dynamic sustainability requires a holistic, realistic and balanced perspective to determine the bad in the good and the good in the bad. However, the idea of embracing such paradoxes in management may be difficult to implement due to various reasons that include individual or organizational path dependence and mental or institutional inertia and resistance. Still, having a new way of thinking is a good first step toward reforming the way of doing. In that sense, incorporating FM and SM into traditional SWOT analysis is a worthwhile exercise that can help us to open an innovative 'window of opportunity,' thereby creating more balanced organ-izational dynamics.

SELECTED BIBLIOGRAPHY

For the operational definitions of success and failure and failure management (FM), see: Lee, J., & Miesing, P. (2017). How Entrepreneurs Can Benefit from Failure Management. *Organizational Dynamics*, 46(3), 157−164. https://doi.org/ 10.1016/j.orgdyn.2017.03.001; Lee, J. (2018). Making Hindsight Foresight: Strategies and Preparedness of Failure Management. *Organizational Dynamics*, 47(3), 165−173. https://doi.org/ 10.1016/j.orgdyn.2017.12.002.

For the success management (SM), see: Lee, J., & Lee, S.-J. (2018). Success Management: Dynamic Sustainability beyond Harms of Success. *Organizational Dynamics*, 47(4), 209−218. https://doi.org/10.1016/j.orgdyn.2018.09.004.

For the SWOT analysis, see: Humphrey, A. (December 2005). SWOT Analysis for Management Consulting. *SRI Alumni Newsletter*. SRI International.

For the 'judo management,' see: Yoffie, D. B., & Cusumano, M. A. (1999). Judo Strategy: The Competitive Dynamics of Internet Time. *Harvard Business Review*, 77(1), 70−81.

CHAPTER **05 Paradox management***
: Challenges and alternatives of organizations' failure-success management

Junesoo Lee

INTRODUCTION

Organizational management is dynamic by nature because of the two paradoxes: (1) organizational failure can be beneficial by cre-ating new opportunities, and (2) organizational success can be harmful by bringing in new crises. The former is the essence of failure management (FM), which asserts that organizational failure and adversity can be positively utilized. The latter is the principle of success management (SM), which emphasizes that the negative aftermath of success should be cautious about. The two approaches (FM and SM; FSM in short) help us recognize and manage a dynamic

---

* To cite the original manuscript of this chapter, use this reference: Lee, J. (2023). Paradox Management: Challenges and Alternatives of Organizations' Failure-Success Management. *KDI School Working Paper Series, 23-16.*

sustainability through paradoxes in our organizations.

However, implementing the failure-success management (FSM) in organizations is easier said than done because there are various obstacles in and out of the organization. Internal and external stakeholders of organizations have many reasons to resist FSM, ranging from psychological hesitation and cultural prematurity to institutional setback and stakeholders' conflict. With this in mind, this article examines the patterns and logic of the challenges of FSM, and introduces theoretical and practical alternatives to sustain FSM in organizations. In the next section, the concepts of FSM are introduced first. Then the challenges and alternatives for effective FSM will follow.

MANAGING ORGANIZATIONAL PARADOXES
: FAILURE-SUCCESS MANAGEMENT

Failure Management (FM)

As previously mentioned, failure management (FM) offers a unique perspective on organizational failures and adversities, viewing them as valuable assets that can help correct errors or explore new opportunities. Failure is defined as a state in which an organization falls short of its goals or expectations, ranging from minor mistakes to significant profit losses or even bankruptcy, which are less desirable than expected outcomes. FM is an optimistic approach that is not limited to the internal affairs of an organization, but also includes both internal and external stakeholders.

When FM is focused on internal stakeholders, such as employees who experience failures, it encourages them to learn from their mistakes and make the most of them. Adopting FM in organizations signals that the organization is led by an entrepreneurial spirit that values experimentalism and views failures as a test-bed and learning opportunity. Consequently, the organization may benefit from increased agility and resiliency, both symbolically and practically.

When FM is applied to external stakeholders, such as customers or beneficiaries, it provides them with a "repechage," i.e., a second chance to recover from their failures. For example, many public or private financial institutions offer debt relief programs to their customers or citizens, adopting this approach. Governments also adopt FM through public service programs such as unemployment benefits or the public service loan forgiveness (PSLF), allowing their citizens more opportunities for a second chance after adversity.

Success Management (SM)

As opposed to FM, which focuses on the bright side of failure, SM looks at the dark side of success. While success is desirable, it can lead to two types of adversity. First, success can cause us to become anchored in our ways of thinking and working, eventually leading to biased decision-making. Second, success can cause external stakeholders, such as customers and rivals, to view our successes in a distorted way, and to become flatterers or predators, which can again impair our decision-making abilities. To avoid these negative consequences of success, we need to more prudently manage the resources and outcomes of success.

Similar to FM, SM can also be used for both internal and external stakeholders. When SM is applied to internal affairs of an organization, providing employees with preventive measures is essential to enable better self-control over resources and powers. Examples include implementing a decision-making process that requires a participatory governance system, or a knowledge management system that stores and shares information on the negative impacts of success to help employees avoid a success trap.

When SM is applied to external stakeholders, such as customers or citizens, many options are available. For instance, many developed countries mandate regular health checks for their citizens to prevent overconfidence in health. Another example is the risk warning provided by financial institutions to their customers, stating, "This product involves a risk of losing your investment principal, so please make a careful decision." A similar approach is taken with lottery winners, who are provided with education on asset management to prevent them from squandering their fortunes. Overall, regulatory measures that aim to mitigate the adverse effects of success may be seen as frustrating, but they actually benefit us by protecting us from being victims of success.

CHALLENGES OF ORGANIZATIONS' FAILURE MANAGEMENT

As previously discussed, FM and SM can be applied to both internal and external stakeholders of organizations. FM can help

Table 1   Challenges of organizations' failure-success management (FSM)

		Internal FSM	External FSM
Main ideas		Helping internal stakeholders' FSM	Helping external stakeholders' FSM
Challenges	FM	**Failure is not an option**: Failure not tolerated in reality	**We have diverse definitions of sustainability**: Static vs. dynamic; micro vs. macro
		Failure is a virtuous evil: Failure management as an excuse of failure	**We have diverse definitions of justice**: Fairness of giving a second chance
	SM	**We lack organizational learning**: Deficient effort to share precaution	**Your SM is none of my business**: Insensitivity to external stakeholders' risks
		We overdo organizational learning: Excessively precautious measures	**My SM is none of your business**: Resistance to external precautious helps

internal and external stakeholders utilize the positive outcomes of failure, whereas SM can help them avoid the negative outcomes of success. However, in practice, the adoption of failure-success management (FSM) is not as simple as one might expect due to many challenges in terms of psychological, relational, cultural, and institutional aspects. First, this section presents the challenges of FM, as summarized in Table 1.

Failure Is Not an Option

There are many popular proverbs and slogans that contain messages of FM, such as "Every cloud has a silver lining," "Every crisis is an opportunity," "Failure is the mother of invention," and "Failure is encouraged in our company," which praise the value of FM. These messages on risk-taking entrepreneurship are often echoed by CEOs and practitioners because the propositions provide not only principles of failure management but also a positive corporate identity that can be beneficial to a company's public relations. However, in reality, failures are not simply tolerated in organizations, and the slogans advocating failure are often limited to rhetoric. The limited adoption of FM in organizations can be attributed to various reasons such as lack of CEO's attention and support, absence of incentives or rewards for utilizing failure, and fear of inflexible performance evaluation or auditing. Consequently, organizational members may feel confused by the ambivalent images of 'proactiveness toward failure,' i.e., a dilemma between 'gamble' and 'experiment'. Thus, the internal environment that opposes FM leads to a cynical organizational culture that questions the real value of FM.

Failure Is a Virtuous Evil

Another adverse reality of FM for internal stakeholders is quite different from the previous one. While the sentiment of "Failure is not an option" is against failure, the view of "Failure is a virtuous evil" goes for failure beyond the pale. The most desirable state for organizations adopting FM might be an institutionalized celebration of failure, which can effectively lead to new insights and discoveries for the future, thanks to failure. However, if the optimistic view on failure goes too far, the organization might be accused of being naïve and negligent because it can make FM an excuse for failure. Such overextended views on failure that exempt every failure without a rigorous and balanced analysis of the positive and negative consequences of failure would be rather detrimental to a healthy organizational culture for FM.

We Have Diverse Definitions of Sustainability

The two previous statements "Failure is not on option," and "Failure is a virtuous evil" are about the resistance to FM for internal stakeholders of organizations. However, there are different challenges when FM is applied to external stakeholders. FM is a way to turn adversity into opportunity, but in the process of transformation, there are diverse and often competing paths of change that can be chosen, and the direction of the change is what really matters to stakeholders. For example, a financial difficulty in an organization can lead to structural or human resource reforms, but the direction of the change can be a source of conflict. It is often said that, for instance, the recent large-scale layoffs in the tech industry can facilitate the redistribution of human resources across the entire industries but can also lead to resentment from those who were laid off. This presents conflicting ideas of sustainability—individual sustainability versus industry sustainability. Competing ideas on sustainability, whether static or dynamic, micro or macro, among stakeholders can create barriers to reform through FM.

We Have Diverse Definitions of Justice

A different barrier to FM, but similar in nature to the previous one, is the varying definitions of justice. FM aims to give a second chance to those who have failed, but this can be seen as unfair by some people. Many ordinary individuals try to avoid failure and accept the consequences if they do fail. However, if the generosity of FM goes beyond certain limits, it can conflict with the principles of justice. For example, some people oppose public policies or financial institutions' measures that forgive debt because they believe it violates their definition of justice, which involves a balance between giving and taking. Similar resentment can also be found in the debate over unemployment benefits, which some see as another infringement on justice. Generally speaking, even when we can agree on a common definition of justice as a "balance," the objects of balance may vary: give and take; give and give; take and take; or any fractional combinations of give and take (for example, give/take and give/take). In short, despite the creative and constructive image, in reality FM can confront various frictions among diverse interests and perspective inside and outside organizations.

CHALLENGES OF ORGANIZATIONS' SUCCESS MANAGEMENT

Success management (SM) is a systematic approach to recognize and mitigate the negative consequences of success. It involves im-plementing measures to prevent biased decision-making within organizations or to avoid negative reactions from external stakeholders. However, implementing SM within organizations is just as challenging as FM due to various barriers such as psycho-logical, cultural, and institutional factors.

We Lack Organizational Learning

To effectively implement SM, one of the most important steps is to learn about the causes and effects of success. In other words, looking back on past experiences, where we have first or sec-ond-hand knowledge of the negative impacts of success, should form the basis of SM. This knowledge of the dark side of success needs to be shared with others in the organization so that we can protect ourselves from being trapped by success. This process of acquiring and sharing knowledge about the adversity generated by success is a process of organizational learning that can lead to better foresight and protective measures.

However, there are many barriers to organizational learning about SM in reality. Firstly, organizational personnel systems often require employees to be transferred to other departments for two purposes: (1) HRD purposes to promote employees' general and universal capabilities, and (2) HRM purposes to equally distribute the advantages and disadvantages of various tasks in organizations. However, the result of the rotational personnel system is inconsistency of work, which can eventually harm effective organizational learning. Secondly, the inflexibility of organizational performance systems can create two kinds of fears among employees: (1) fear of disclosing my discredit, and (2) fear of disclosing others' credit. The consequence of these fears is a lack of trust in the "fair trade" of organizational memory. In other words, unless people have a sense of fair exchange of giving (knowledge sharing) and taking (compensation), people's know-how on SM cannot be stored, transferred, and shared in organizations. Thirdly, even when employees know and comply with the spirit of knowledge sharing on SM, they may be unable to participate in sharing because they lack methods or media to store and transfer their knowledge and experience on SM. As a result of these three stumbling blocks to organizational learning, the valuable experiences of SM cannot become a part of the organizational asset.

We Overdo Organizational Learning

On the contrary to the lack of organizational learning, sometimes we experience the opposite pattern of organizational change. Especially during a serious crisis in organizations or when a new CEO takes office, we often witness a dramatic change across all parts of the organization. Excessive precautionary measures, too many new standards or manuals, or undue structural changes are some examples that we can call "reform fever." This represents unnecessary reforms that take place not only for effective change but also for a euphoric feeling of change. The results of such overstepped changes include a "manual flood" or a "standardization trap," where some preventive measures are originally designed to protect us from the negative impacts of success but actually entrap us in reality.

Your Success Management Is None of My Business

The two previously discussed phenomena of SM—deficiency and excess of organizational learning—are targeted on internal stake-holders of organizations. However, when SM is directed towards external stakeholders such as customers or citizens, there are other types of challenges that arise. If an organization wants to assist its customers in SM, there can be resistance from within the organization. For instance, as discussed previously, many manu-facturers or financial institutions provide their customers with risk warnings in various forms, such as alert messages or contract terms, to help customers avoid moral hazards or ignorance of risks after experiencing the benefits of products or services. Governments also enact a broad range of regulations, such as regular checkups and mandatory education, to safeguard citizens from being trapped by success. However, such SM-based measures for customers or citizens can only be implemented when organizations are sensitive to the risks faced by external stakeholders. Unfortunately, organizations often lack significant attention to the risks faced by their customers because a customer's success occurs today certainly, but a failure due to that success may occur uncertainly in the future. In short, an organization's internal insensitivity to its constituency's risks hinders the organization's SM for external stakeholders.

The two phenomena mentioned above, "We overdo organizational learning" and "Your success management is none of my business," embody two distinct aspects of the "power game," which involves competition for power and influence among various stakeholders and groups. Specifically, the former phenomenon, "We overdo organizational learning," exemplifies the "pulling game" in which we strive for more authority and resources, engage in popular activities excessively, and consequently become overly active. On the other hand, the latter phenomenon, "Your success management is none of my business," arises from the "pushing game" where we vie for less responsibility and risks, avoid unpopular activities, and ultimately become inactive.

My Success Management Is None of Your business

When an organization tries to protect its external stakeholders who may experience risks due to success, the targeted external stakeholders may resist the protective measures and precautions. Typically, we tend to ignore any risks until they become apparent, especially if the risks are an unexpected negative outcome of a delightful success. For instance, a healthy person may be over-confident about any health risks and neglect the importance of regular checkups. Similarly, a successful business can make owners and employees unrealistically optimistic about their capabilities responding to the future market situation. This biased perception and assessment of future risks due to success may result in insufficient attention to and resistance to external support and interventions for SM. Instances of such external stakeholders' resistance to SM due to their overconfidence are abundant, including low participation in regular checkups or vaccination campaigns, low turnout in public education, and high violation of the warning terms in insurance contracts.

ALTERNATIVES FOR ORGANIZATIONS' CHALLENGES OF FAILURE-SUCCESS MANAGEMENT

The challenges of organizational FSM discussed in the previous sections represent a gap between the theory and practice of FSM. In theory, it is desirable for organizations to employ FSM perspectives to systematically manage organizational paradoxes. However, the implementation of FSM is confronted by many practical challenges. Nonetheless, we need breakthroughs to overcome these challenges; otherwise, the managerial paradoxes—the positive impacts of failure and the negative impacts of success —will remain unaddressed and undeveloped. Thus, this section presents a set of good practices and principles that can help us better deal with the challenges of organizational FSM.

Alternatives for the FSM Challenges: 5W1H Approach

To address the challenges of FSM, there are various methodologies that can be employed. This article adopts a 5W1H (WHAT, WHO, WHEN, WHERE, WHY, HOW) approach that provides a logical description and systematic prescription for FSM. Table 2 highlights the first three elements (WHY, WHAT, HOW) of FSM alternatives. WHY represents the rationale for the need for breakthroughs in organizational FSM, as previously discussed. WHAT refers to the core actions that need to be taken to embrace FSM in organizations. HOW includes the specific methods that can be employed to implement these actions. In summary, as there are four groups of challenges—internal FM, external FM, internal SM, external SM— there should be four corresponding alternative perspectives.

First, the challenges of internal FM stem from viewing failure either as an unbearable thing or as an easy excuse for fallacy. Both approaches lack "rigorous tolerance." Failure should be tolerated to constructively revisit it as a valuable asset, but such positive analysis of failure still needs to be conducted rigorously to avoid naïve negligence. Therefore, overcoming the challenges of internal FM is to *capitalize outcomes of failure through rigorous tolerance.*

Second, the challenges of external FM originate from diverse definitions and interests regarding the "second chance" for those who fail. Competing values on sustainability and justice represent different stakeholders' cherished values. One way to resolve such dilemmas is to apply competing values to different spaces and times. For instance, giving a second chance to losers may not always be justified but can be acceptable when the loss occurs in a risky business where every employee hesitates to work. Thus, handling the challenge of external FM is to *balance competing values through complementary diversification.*

Third, the challenges of internal SM arise from inadequate organizational learning. Organizational memory on the negative

Table 2 Alternatives for the challenges of organizations' failure-success management (FSM)

		Internal FSM	External FSM
Main ideas		Helping internal stakeholders' FSM	Helping external stakeholders' FSM
WHY (challenges)	FM	**Failure is not an option:** Failure not tolerated in reality	**We have diverse definitions of sustainability:** Static vs. dynamic; micro vs. macro
		Failure is a virtuous evil: Failure management as an excuse of failure	**We have diverse definitions of justice:** Fairness of giving a second chance
		Alternative WHAT: **Capitalize outcomes of failure** HOW: **Through rigorous tolerance**	Alternative WHAT: **Balance competing values** HOW: **Through complementary diversification**
	SM	**We lack organizational learning:** Deficient effort to share precaution	**Your SM is none of my business:** Insensitivity to external stakeholders' risks
		We overdo organizational learning: Excessively precautious measures	**My SM is none of your business:** Resistance to external precautious helps
		Alternative WHAT: **Systemize caution of success** HOW: **Through accountable learning**	Alternative WHAT: **Internalize external risks and helps** HOW: **Through empathic collaboration**

impacts of success and the know-how to overcome such para-doxical outcomes of success is challenging to store and share. To promote SM, we need to institutionalize learning and sharing efforts of SM by promoting a sense of accountability to protect ourselves and our neighbors from the success trap. Therefore, dealing with the challenge of internal SM is to *systemize caution of success through accountable learning.*

Fourth, the challenges of external SM are based on ignorance of others' risks due to their success and negligence of our own risks due to our success. The common factor behind these challenges is a lack of sensitivity to the dark side of success. To overcome such inactivity, we need empathy with the victims of success to internalize their risks as our own, as well as humility to accept and comply with external help. Thus, the method of managing the challenge of external SM is to *internalize external risks and helps through empathic collaboration.*

The four statements previously mentioned represent the three items (WHY, WHAT, HOW) among the 5W1H alternatives for the challenges of FSM. To make them more valid and implement-

Table 3 Organizational platforms for failure-success management (FSM)

WHO (subject of FSM): Collectivity level	WHEN/WHERE (space-time context of FSM): Value integration level	
	Low (emerging, open, free, inclusive, diverse, unofficial)	High (deliberate, closed, rigorous, selective, integrative, official)
Low (individual)	**Knowledge (holistic) creation** (e.g., knowledge creator's sandbox)	**Knowledge (active) transfer** (e.g., systemized hand-over)
High (group)	**Knowledge (passive) sharing** (e.g., Failcon, Failexpo)	**Knowledge (systematic) application** (e.g., institutionalized experimentalism)

able, these statements should be specified and supported by the remaining three items (WHO, WHEN, WHERE). Table 3 presents a way to systemize the alternatives by applying two dimensions. The first dimension is WHO, which concerns the subject of FSM in organizations and can be categorized based on the collectivity level into individual and group level. The second dimension is WHEN and WHERE, which represents the space and time context of FSM in organizations and can be divided into two categories (low and high) based on the level of value integration. A low level of value integration is conducted in an emerging, open, free, inclusive, diverse, and unofficial environment, whereas a high level of value integration is done in a deliberate, closed, rigorous, selective, integrative, and official setting. By combining the two dimensions that have two categories, the matrix generates four cells repre-senting the four organizational platforms for FSM. These platforms can help secure, align, and facilitate FSM in terms of leadership, culture, and institutions of organizations.

FSM Platform for Knowledge (Holistic) Creation

The starting point for implementing FSM in organizations is an individual who perceives the paradoxes of failure and success and enforces measures to handle them. Only when individuals exercise FSM, knowledge and practices of FSM can be stored, shared, and utilized across the organization. Therefore, individuals should be the fundamental basis of knowledge creation for FSM. However, knowledge creation is not automatic. Employees need certain conditions to seek, find, and create knowledge on FSM.

First, individuals should have a sense of being in a "fear-free zone" for learning. Both those who fail and those who succeed need an organizational environment to reflect on the paradoxes they experience and how they handle them without fear of being falsely accused. Second, they need useful learning methods that help them find patterns of problems and solutions of failure and success. A set of holistic methods, such as Benchmarking, Modeling, Forecasting, and Backcasting (BMFB), might be helpful. Benchmarking involves collecting good and bad practices and identifying critical factors of success and failure. Modeling is used to find generalizable patterns and causalities behind the success/failure factors. Forecasting predicts the future based on legitimate models, while backcasting involves creating actionable plans to reach the future predicted.

When at least two conditions, i.e., a comfortable learning atmosphere and holistic learning methods, are satisfied, individuals can benefit from a "knowledge creator's sandbox," where they are free to experiment and create novel knowledge on the paradoxes without fear of accusations or ignorance. As a result, individuals who acquire knowledge on FSM can transform their implicit experiences into explicit knowledge by creating their own database, which can range from a simple memo to a more comprehensive manual, toolkit, or handbook for FSM.

FSM Platform for Knowledge (Passive) Sharing

The FSM knowledge created by individuals should be shared and diffused to benefit organizations. However, sharing knowledge beyond individuals can be challenging due to several barriers, such as fear of ridicule or criticism from others, and a lack of sharing opportunities or venues. Therefore, the "fear-free zone" needs to be expanded beyond individual learning to form a learning community.

One example of a learning community for FSM is Failcon (thefailcon.com), a US-based enterprise that regularly holds conferences where entrepreneurs who have experienced failure and success in their businesses can gather to share their experiences. Such gatherings have enormous benefits because they take on a festive atmosphere, making it easier for people to share their know-how of business paradoxes without fear of any official penalty in their organizations. South Korea has a similar model, where the Ministry of the Interior and Safety hosts an annual meeting called "Failexpo" for citizens and organizations to share their stories of failure and success, with similarly positive results.

Participants in such public venues for sharing FSM knowledge do not have to be present at the same place and time. Beyond close and synchronized contact, remote and asynchronous meetings can be gathered via digital cloud systems where people can leave and access stories and knowledge of FSM without limits of time and space.

All these methods of sharing FSM knowledge have the characteristics of an open, free, and unofficial learning community. However, the open and free attribute of the method is like a double-edged sword. Although participants are not obligated to join or exchange their ideas, there is no guarantee that organizations would manage the valuable knowledge systematically, so that they can eventually benefit from it. Therefore, we need another method of officially transferring knowledge of FSM within organizations, which is introduced in the next section.

FSM Platform for Knowledge (Active) Transfer

The aforementioned method of knowledge sharing is to provide an open and free venue where people may freely exchange their ideas on FSM, enabling a learning community to be formed. However, as knowledge related to FSM often remains as intangible and unstable asset of an organization, we need another reliable method to ensure knowledge transfer within organizations. In specific, considering the typical personnel system where em-ployees are regularly transferred to other departments for HRD and HRM purposes, we must build a more systematic handover system that allows FSM knowledge to be shared between the predecessor and successor of every position in the organization.

An example from South Korea can show a model of such FSM knowledge transfer among the staff. The South Korean government manages an online system called the "On-nara service," a comprehensive and integrative online platform for documentation and communication. The system accommodates various demands on internal affairs such as documentation and communication with internal and external stakeholders through email, chat, and video conference. What makes the system unique is its knowledge management function. Government officials can join online bulletins and learning communities to share their ideas. Furthermore, the system includes a handover section through which information and knowledge can be systematically transferred from predecessor to successor of any position. The forms of knowledge transferred between officials vary from explicit, such as formal and official data, information, and documents, to implicit, such as informal and unofficial data and information like video clips, memos, checklists, handbooks, and manuals that contain any know-how on works. In doing so, the volatile and intangible knowledge on FSM can be formally saved and enriched, constituting institutional assets.

FSM Platform for Knowledge (Systematic) Application

All the methods previously mentioned provide venues for creating and sharing knowledge of FSM. However, to effectively connect the shared knowledge to organizational outcomes, the efforts towards FSM need to be institutionalized into the decision -making process. As the essence of FSM is to systematically respond to the paradoxical impacts of failure and success by learning from trials and errors in organizations, the experimentalism should become a part of the organizational procedure and culture. In other words, we need to ensure a "down-to-earth zone" as well as a "fear-free zone" in our organizations, through which all organizational experiences of failure and success can be trans- formed into practical lessons and insightful decision-making.

In fact, FSM is not far away from our daily lives in organizations. All businesses and policies in our organizations are not only the goals we try to achieve today but also the means, rehearsal, test, and experiment for the next level's goals we want to achieve tomorrow. Therefore, an organizational attitude and policy towards experimentalism for FSM will lead to a more audacious and proactive organizational culture. Organizational proactivity can be defined in various ways. As Table 4 presents, an

Figure 1 Measures for organizational proactivity towards effective FSM

External participation

- Reporting good (success) and bad (failure) practices
- Proposing new practices for FSM
- Engaging in participatory governance

Protection of proactivity
(exemption, insurance)

Ex-ante
measures

Promotion of proactivity
(incentives, rewards, HRD)

Ex-post
measures

Prevention of inactivity
(monitoring, penalty)

Internal supports

- Establishing a legal basis to protect and promote FSM
- Providing counseling and consulting services for FSM
- Managing praticipatory governance

organization's proactivity can manifest multidimensionally, ranging from discomfort solution and problem prevention to performance improvement and innovation exploration.

In any types of proactivity, in order to make organizations more proactive towards effective FSM, a set of multifaceted measures must be taken. Figure 1 illustrates three types of actions for organizational proactivity: (1) prevention of inactivity through

Table 4. Types of organizational proactivity

Temporal focus	Directional focus	
	Minimizing bad	Maximizing good
Retrospective (reflectional, reactive)	**Discomfort solution**	**Performance improvement**
Prospective (preventive, anticipatory)	**Problem prevention**	**Innovation exploration**

monitoring and penalties; (2) promotion of proactivity through incentives, rewards, and HRD systems; and (3) protection of proactivity through exemption from penalties and insurance for audacious and creative failures. These actions can be further promoted with the help of both internal and external stakeholders. External stakeholders, such as customers and citizens, can contribute to organizational proactivity by: (1) reporting both good (success) and bad (failure) practices of an organization; (2) proposing new practices for handling success and failure; and (3) participating in governance processes within the organization. Internal stakeholders, including CEOs and higher management, can promote organizational FSM by: (1) establishing a legal basis to protect and promote FSM; (2) providing counseling and consulting services for FSM; and (3) managing participatory governance within the organization. In summary, taking the measures for organizational proactivity will also promote effective FSM.

CONCLUSION: DYNAMIC SUSTAINABILITY THROUGH PARADOXES

Organizational management is inherently dynamic, especially due to two paradoxes: (1) failure can sometimes have positive out-comes by creating new opportunities, and (2) success can some-times be negative by bringing in new crises. Dealing with such two paradoxes, failure management (FM) and success management (SM) can help manage these paradoxical phenomena. However, implementing the failure-success management (FSM) in organizations can be challenging due to various obstacles and resistance from inside and outside the organization. This article examined the patterns and logic of these challenges and introduced theoretical and practical alternatives to sustain FSM in organizations.

No matter what smart strategies and tactics for FSM are suggested, it is ultimately up to us to actually design and implement them in our organizations. One of the ultimate factors that help us effectively realize FSM might be the organizational mission. In other words, a constant awareness of the answers to two questions on the organizational mission, (1) who we are; and (2) who we (have to) serve, will be a lighthouse or guiding hand that lead us to the dynamic sustainability through paradoxes. Then, how can we have such constant awareness of our mission? We do not have to worry so much about it, because organizational failures and adversities will play their paradoxical roles as a reminder of the organizational mission. In other words, organizational difficulties will function as micro and temporary disequilibrium that leads to macro and ultimate equilibrium. That is an organizational paradox that leads us to dynamic sustainability.

SELECTED
BIBLIOGRAPHY

For failure management and success management, see: Lee, J., & Miesing, P. (2017). How Entrepreneurs Can Benefit from Failure Management. *Organizational Dynamics*, 46(3), 157−164; Lee, J. (2018). Making Hindsight Foresight: Strategies and Preparedness of Failure Management. Organizational Dynamics, 47(3), 165−173; Lee, J., & Lee, S.-J. (2018). Success Management: Dynamic Sustainability beyond Harms of Success. Organizational Dynamics, 47(4), 209−218; and Lee, J., Lee, S.-J., & Jung, K. (2020). Balanced SWOT: Revisiting SWOT Analysis through Failure Management and Success Management. *KDI School Working Paper Series, 20−17.*

For sustainability (static vs. dynamic; micro vs. macro), see: Lee, J. (2024). Sustainable Paradise Lost: Competing and Complementary Discussions on Sustainability. *Environment, Development and Sustainability.* https://doi.org/10.1007/s10668−024−04711−5.

For BMFB (benchmarking, modeling, forecasting, backcasting) and the remote and a−synchronized learning community, see: Lee, J. (2023). The Era of Omni−learning: Frameworks and Practices of the Expanded Human Resource Development. *Organizational Dynamics*, 52(1), 100916.

For the comprehensive theories and practices of knowledge management, see: Dalkir, K. (2017). *Knowledge Management in Theory and Practice* (3rd edition). The MIT Press; and Hislop, D., Bosua, R., & Helms, R. (2018). *Knowledge Management in Organizations: A Critical Introduction* (4th edition). Oxford University Press.

For the organizational proactivity, see: *Recognizing Proactive Governance Best Practices*. Ministry of Personnel Management. https://www.mpm.go.kr/proactivePublicServiceEn

Epilogue

This book introduces Failure Management (FM) and Success Management (SM) as methods to systematically recognize and manage the paradoxical and sometimes perplexing experiences brought by failure and success. In essense, considering the co-existence of signal and noise in our world, FM is an appreciation of signal not only AMONG noises but also IN noise (i.e., noise as signal), whereas SM is a (pre)caution of signal as potential noise (i.e., signal as noise).

However, these methods of Failure/Success Management (collectively referred to as FSM) do not imply that we can fully control failures and successes and their paradoxical impacts. Instead, as we experience the uncontrollable and mysteriously paradoxical influences of failure and success, we intuitively realize that such events occur with a certain purpose. Another expression of this purpose is 'mission,' indicating that failures and successes guide us to realize and follow a certain mission.

In this context, we can consider two types of missions. The

first is the 'mission to me,' which concerns how I should live as an individual entity, and the second is the 'mission through me,' which concerns how I should interact with my neighbors and the world. Summarizing the core values of these two missions, we interestingly discover common initial consonants in Korean words that are meaningfully connected. The first is ㅅㄹ, the initials for love (사랑) and shalom (샬롬) (meaning peace, harmony, tranquility). The second is ㄱㅅ, the initials for humility (겸손) and gratitude (감사). The first consonant pair, ㅅㄹ, represents the ultimate values we aim for, while the second pair, ㄱㅅ, represents the methodological values that guide us toward those ultimate values.

Now, reflecting from the perspective of Failure/Success Management, failure and success compel us to introspect and reflect at personal, organizational, and societal levels, inevitably leading to continuous change and innovation. Ultimately, we find that failure and success urge and assist us in embodying and aspiring toward better 'ㅅㄹ' (love, shalom) and 'ㄱㅅ' (humility, gratitude). In the rollercoaster of emotions of failure and success, we experience the DS (dynamic sustainability; dynamic shalom), and our belief in such a paradoxical providence brings us comfort and hope.

Index

nudge   13, 14, 28

O
objective   82, 83, 87, 96, 102, 119

objectives   71, 78, 96, 121

operating system   64

opportunity   11, 12, 19, 24, 38, 39,
   40, 96, 99, 100, 107, 110, 117,
   118, 119, 121, 125, 128, 130

optimistic   63, 65, 129

organizational learning   127, 132,
   133, 134, 135, 138

OS X(10)   10

Oulu   19

outflanking   42, 44, 45, 56, 100,
   112

overconfidence   61, 63, 66, 67, 93,
   119, 126

overestimate   63, 64

Oxfam   46

P
paradox   6, 23, 24, 27, 34, 61, 65,
   86, 93, 97, 98, 102, 103, 104,
   105, 120, 121, 123, 124, 137, 141,
   142, 143, 146, 148, 149, 153, 154

path dependence   121

PDA   71

Peace First   17

Pepsi   13

perfect game   87

planful opportunism   86, 94

planned FM   49, 50, 51, 55, 57,
   100, 108

Polaroid   75

Porras   43, 58, 94

portfolio   2, 23, 70

positioning   70, 79

Post-it note   33, 44, 51, 54, 86,
   108, 109, 113

power game   135

prepared FM   49, 52, 53, 55, 57,
   100, 111

proactivity   147, 148, 151

Procter & Gamble   83

proposition   7, 10, 22, 24, 35, 98,
   99, 101

prospective   1, 5, 6, 24, 27, 34, 36,
   40, 56

pulling game   135

R
re-anchoring   42, 45, 56, 100, 108,
   113

reform   9, 43, 64, 84, 99, 121, 130,
   134

reform fever   134

reinforce   63, 64, 75

repechage   125

resource curse   86

68, 95, 96, 97, 98, 99, 104, 105, 106, 107, 110, 111, 112, 113, 120

3M   33, 44, 83, 86, 108, 109

Tim Cook   18

time horizon   51, 54, 55, 57

Toyota   16

trial and error   2, 44, 53

Trinity Alliance   17

Tropical Islands Resort   12

tunnel vision   56, 64

U

Uber   12

uncertainty   23, 27, 51, 55

unique   7, 43, 61, 74, 98, 117, 124

(the) UK   21

(the) US   21, 67, 76, 109, 110, 111, 114

(the) USSR   33, 42, 45

unprecedented   48, 110

unstable equilibrium   30

V

vaccine   45

value   18, 20, 35, 37, 38, 39, 40, 43, 46, 50, 54, 58, 79, 80, 81, 83, 91, 102, 109, 112, 115, 125, 128, 129, 138, 141, 154

value chain   35, 37, 38, 39, 40, 58, 79

variable   10, 23, 91

W

Walgreens   84, 85

Wang(Laboratories)   70, 71, 75

weakness   56, 76, 95, 97, 98, 102, 104, 105, 106, 107, 108, 109, 111, 112, 113, 120

Westinghouse   65

winner's curse   62

Winston Churchill   45, 83, 118, 119

Y

Yin-Yang   94

Yuri Gagarin   109

Authors

Junesoo Lee is a Professor at the KDI School of Public Policy and Management, in charge of the Dynamic Sustainability Laboratory (DS Lab). He received his PhD in Public Administration and Policy from the State University of New York at Albany. His research focuses on paradox management through dynamic sustainability, where systems can be sustained by beneficial failure (i.e., failure management) and also challenged by harmful success (i.e., success management).

Paul Miesing is the Founding Director of UAlbany's Center for Advancement and Understanding of Social Enterprises (CAUSE) at the State University of New York at Albany. He received his PhD in Strategic Management from the University of Colorado at Boulder. His current research interests are in social entrepreneurship, environmental sustainability, and corporate governance. He has published dozens of articles and papers in both academic and practitioner journals, most recently co-editing Educating Social Entrepreneurs: A Workbook of Cases, Exercises, and Commentaries (Principles for Responsible Management Education). Prof. Miesing was a Fulbright lecturer at Fudan University in Shanghai, has won numerous awards and recognitions, and served on several peer review boards.

Seung-Joo Lee is a Professor at the KDI School of Public Policy and Management and Associate Dean of the Center for International Cooperation and Capacity Building. He received his DBA from Harvard University and worked at McKinsey & Co. as a management consultant. He conducts research on global megatrends and teaches in the areas of strategic management, entrepreneurship, and leadership.

Kwon Jung is a Professor at the KDI School of Public Policy and Management and Associate Dean of the Office of Planning and External Affairs. He received his Ph.D. in Marketing at the University of Illinois at Urbana-Champaign. His research interest lies in understanding consumer behaviors in both private and public sectors and sustainable business strategy.

2nd edition

Failure Management & Success Management

Published the second edition in 2024. 7. 25
Published the first edition in 2021. 8. 10

Author	Junesoo Lee · Paul Miesing · Seung-Joo Lee · Kwon Jung
President	Jong-Man An · Sang-Joon An
Publishing Company	Parkyoung Publishing & Company
	#210, 53, Gasan digital 2-ro, Geumcheon-gu, Seoul
	Registered in 1959.3.11. 300-1959-1
tel	82-2-733-6771
fax	82-2-736-4818
e-mail	pys@pybook.co.kr
homepage	www.pybook.co.kr
ISBN	979-11-303-2044-1 93320

15,000₩ (Korean Currency)